The Empire God Built

The Empire God Built

Inside Pat Robertson's Media Machine

ALEC FOEGE

John Wiley & Sons, Inc.

New York · Chichester · Brisbane · Toronto · Singapore

For Erica

Contents

CHAPTER 6

On the Air—Thursday Morning, March 21, 1996,
Studio 7, Virginia Beach, Virginia

75

CHAPTER 7

The Club

81

CHAPTER 8

On the Air—At the 1992 Republican National Convention,
Houston, Texas, August 19, 1992

107

CHAPTER 9

The Coalition

115

CHAPTER 10

On the Air—10:00 A.M., April 29, 1994

153

CHAPTER 11

On the Web

163

CHAPTER 12

The University

173

ACKNOWLEDGMENTS

Special thanks are due to the following people for graciously granting interviews for the purposes of this book:

Rob Boston
Edmund Cohen
Kevin Danford
John Dowless
Barbara Handman
David Edwin Harrell Jr.
Jonathan Hudson
Andy Jacobs Jr.
Simon Jaffee
Steve Magnuson
Jon Mandel
Julia Martin
Charles R. McDowell

David Mizner
Matthew W. Paxton III
Skipp Porteous
Jerry Rose
Jay Alan Sekulow
R. Bruce Skewes
Jerry Sloan
Dr. Alan Snyder
Andrew Stettner
Gerard Straub
David Twersky
Mel White

A man of genius has a right to any mode of expression.
—Ezra Pound

Every man thinks God is on his side. The rich and powerful know he is.
—Jean Anouilh

THE EMPIRE

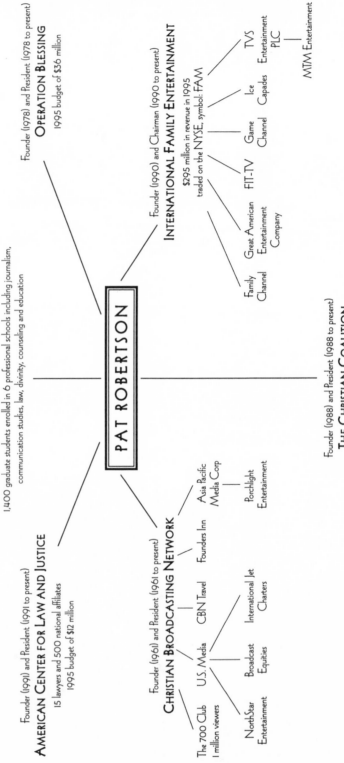

PAT ROBERTSON

Founder (1977) and Chancellor (1977 to present)
REGENT UNIVERSITY

1,400 graduate students enrolled in 6 professional schools including journalism, communication studies, law, divinity, counseling and education

Founder (1978) and President (1978 to present)
OPERATION BLESSING

1995 budget of $36 million

Founder (1990) and Chairman (1990 to present)
INTERNATIONAL FAMILY ENTERTAINMENT

$295 million in revenue in 1995
traded on the NYSE, symbol: FAM

- Family Channel
- Great American Entertainment Company
- FIT-TV
- Game Channel
- Ice Capades
- TVS Entertainment PLC
- MTM Entertainment

Founder (1991) and President (1991 to present)
AMERICAN CENTER FOR LAW AND JUSTICE

15 lawyers and 500 national affiliates
1995 budget of $12 million

Founder (1961) and President (1961 to present)
CHRISTIAN BROADCASTING NETWORK

- The 700 Club
  1 million viewers
- NorthStar Entertainment
- U.S. Media
  - Broadcast Equities
  - International Jet Charters
- CBN Travel
- Founders Inn
- Asia Pacific Media Corp
- Porchlight Entertainment

Founder (1988) and President (1988 to present)
THE CHRISTIAN COALITION

1.7 million members

CHAPTER ONE

The Television

C hannel-surfing has revolutionized television-viewing.

This in itself is hardly news. But recall for a moment the not-so-distant past when TVs had manual dials instead of infrared remote controls and antennas rather than a cable box and a coaxial cord snaking through the side of the house: The contrast between then and now seems drastic and primordial.

Commercial advertising spots—television's raison d'être and main source of income—for many years played to relatively captive audiences. Since TV viewers weren't likely to get up, walk to their sets, and switch channels every single time a three-minute block of ads showed up, advertisers more often than not could count on an attentive consumer. Furthermore, the majority of those viewers/consumers watched the three major networks, ABC, CBS, and NBC. As a result, TV advertising gained legitimacy as a cultural force.

From the 1950s on, a popular mythology filled with characters like the Marlboro Man, the Jolly Green Giant, and Mr. Clean enjoyed vast recognition and currency. Regardless of their message—which was, invariably and simply, to buy green beans or household cleaner or whatever product was being sold—these commercials were successful in lodging their fictional pitchmen in the minds of millions.

It was because of, and not despite, their basic and constant message that these commercials became so memorable. Set free from the need to devise fresh viewpoints or messages, advertising-firm creative departments were able to focus on window dressing. In advertising, concepts, characters, presentation, colors, artwork, and production values comprise the bulk of the creative effort.

And rightly so: Television is reductive; television viewers can be fickle. All programming, regardless of its content or message, has only seconds to establish a mood—a whole environment, really. An up-to-the-minute, appealing look and feel is how one gets noticed.

———◦———

Remote controls and cable television have put this whole system somewhat into question. No longer can advertisers assume that the majority of a program's viewers will stick around for the commercial breaks.

According to the U.S. Census Bureau, a whopping 61 percent of United States households with televisions in 1993 received cable TV, as compared with a mere 20 percent in 1980.

With the surfeit of channels provided as part of most basic cable TV packages—mine includes somewhere between 60 and 70, a number that increases and decreases regularly as new ventures start up and old ones fail—and the lightning maneuverability afforded by today's remote controls, one need never again watch another commercial from beginning to end.

Now advertising must compete directly with programming. Why watch a commercial when you can check out the latest video on MTV? Or a news update on CNN? Or an old movie that you haven't seen in years? Or a new movie that you're hoping to catch when it repeats again next week?

This is how I first lit upon *The 700 Club,* Pat Robertson's star vehicle and the flagship broadcast of the Family Channel.

I watch television holding the remote in my right hand. The split second a program I am watching fades into a commercial, my finger glides to a button. In even less time, I'm somewhere new—possibly somewhere related.

Say, I were watching Mary Tyler Moore in *Stolen Memories: Secrets From the Rose Garden,* a recent TV movie starring the 1970s icon as a childlike adult woman getting by in the segregationist South of the 1950s.

The intricate latticework of cable television programming is such that on the commercial breaks I could potentially catch Moore on either *The Dick Van Dyke Show*, the 1960s sitcom where she got her start, *The Mary Tyler Moore Show*, the 1970s sitcom that made her a star, or perhaps even *Ordinary People*, the 1980 movie that established her as a serious dramatic actor.

To me, this channel-hopping has become so natural—almost innate—that I might not even notice that *Stolen Memories* was being broadcast on Pat Robertson's Family Channel, the cable network that funded its production.

A flip to the Family Channel at some other time might uncover a rerun of *Evening Shade* from the reserves of MTM Productions, the production company founded by Moore and her ex-husband, NBC chief Grant Tinker, and now owned by International Family Entertainment, the publicly held corporation chaired by Pat Robertson. (Reruns of *The Mary Tyler Moore Show*, however, are licensed to Nickelodeon, a Family Channel rival, until 2005.)

Each program would be broadcast on a different channel (Nickelodeon, TNT, HBO, or USA perhaps). Each would be most likely discovered at random, piecemeal, and in progress. All would be related, but not due to any broadcaster's master plan.

By stumbling about with my remote control's directional buttons or by punching its numbers or by zapping the last-channel button, I myself find and gather these interrelated programs. With a deft wrist and alert mind, I can create an audiovisual collage that is at once entertaining, informative, and yet blissfully temporary.

Constantly flitting from aisle to aisle (from channel to channel) instead of waiting to see what each aisle might serve up produces a different and heightened viewing experience. Channel surfing is a pointedly apt term for this technique; assembling the most energizing combination of programming bits is indeed something akin to riding the perfect wave.

While I'm watching TV, I tend to lose track of where I started, why I departed, and what I was looking to watch in the first place. Regardless of how interested I am in the first program I settle upon, as soon as the first commercial break arrives (it's rarely more than ten minutes between commercials, frequently closer to five), I surf. When I find another program that appears at least marginally interesting, I stop.

Soon enough, that program will reach an advertising break—or else, after a couple minutes or seconds of viewing I discover either that it's dull, not what I thought it was, or that even a millisecond's lull in the action is more than I can possibly stand.

So I hop back to the first channel. Perhaps the commercials are still running. Time to check the news or the weather. Or if there's a better sitcom or a rare old movie or a new drama series or riveting documentary or the same old music video or a new stock market high or a familiar talk show or a smarmy infomercial or some whole new channel devoted to a specific area of interest. (The Food Network and the Sci-Fi Channel are a couple of the recent additions to my basic package.)

A few hours later, my viewing desires sated, I turn off the tube. Whether I emerge zonked out or relaxed or invigorated, I am quick to realize that I have not watched a single show or movie or music video or commercial in its entirety. And yet I genuinely believe that I have panned my way through a segment of television's endless river of programming, filtered out the dross, and captured only the most valuable nuggets.

Ironically, while the amount of original television programming available at any given time has increased exponentially, the quality of each segment of that programming has stayed about the same (and possibly declined in the case of networks and channels trying to fill voluminous tracts of air time with fresh material but finite budgets and talent pools).

My hunch is that an increasing percentage of viewers watch cable TV the way I do, even if it's only because when one is paying monthly bills for more channels and better reception the instinct is to get one's money's worth. The evolution is a perfectly natural one.

What seems odd is that few networks or programmers have acknowledged this sea change in viewing habits. The original big three—NBC, CBS, and ABC—trudge on in their old, tattered overcoats. Inexplicably, CBS is still referred to as the Tiffany Network, for its supposedly classy programming geared toward older viewers. Never mind that its lineup is virtually indistinguishable from that of its competitors and that 1995 witnessed CBS's worst decline ever.

Even the efforts of Fox, the most recent addition to the network big league, seem futile. Sure, Fox staples like *The Simpsons* and *Married With Children* appeal to a younger, hipper audience, but who outside of the broadcasting business community actually identifies each program with the network that broadcasts it?

Despite the recent startups of two more fledgling networks, Viacom's UPN and Time Warner's WB, the notion of a network devising one roster to fulfill its loyal audience's every need is antiquated and slouching toward obsolescence. According to a 1995 year-end assessment in *The New York Times,* cable-channel viewership was up 10 percent in 1995 as network-television audiences continued to decline.

But cable channels fail to establish identities for a host of different reasons. Due to budgetary considerations, the bulk of the average cable channel's programming is reruns, and it frankly doesn't matter one whit to most viewers whether they watch their favorite sitcoms on the Comedy Channel or on TBS. Those cable channels that pride themselves on original programming must fight the battle of consistently drawing viewers from other channels to their own—the same battle the established networks are losing.

If a viewer, for example, wants to watch old episodes of *The Waltons,* then that viewer will go to whatever channel is showing *The Waltons.* Period.

How many television executives can afford to believe that programming itself no longer guarantees viewers? Better yet, how many broadcasters can afford to make that precept their guiding light?

I know of only one—Pat Robertson. And from that revelation sprung this book.

———◦———

The Family Channel, the cable network founded by Robertson and today run by his son, Timothy, is the eleventh-largest cable-television network in the country. In 1992, the *New York Times* declared the Family Channel "one of the most profitable television channel ever, religious or secular."

For most of the day, the Family Channel broadcasts "classic" television shows—everything from reruns of pabulum children's fare such as

Inspector Gadget, Flintstone Kids, and *Heathcliff* in the morning hours to *The Waltons, Bonanza,* and *Rescue 911* in the evening. Between the reruns and the G-rated movies and country music specials that comprise the programming of most cable channels is *The 700 Club.*

News junkies and political experts should be more than familiar with the basic details of Pat Robertson's rise to power. I don't presume myself to be better informed than the hundreds of journalists who have tracked Robertson over the years. So while this book contains plenty of primary-source reporting and gathers much information that hasn't appeared together in one place before, its ultimate aim is something quite different.

This account of Pat Robertson's personal history and the brave new world he has created will, of course, trigger some of the same warning bells that others have set off before—but it provides a genuinely fresh perspective, as well. By approaching Robertson from all levels—his TV persona, his business activities, his sociopolitical maneuvers, and his personal history—I aim to reveal a cross section of today's communications culture. Virtually the only aspect of Robertson that I do not explore in detail is his religious convictions. Religion is merely the means by which Robertson has achieved his ends.

Pat Robertson's communications achievements are of such magnitude and breadth that a traditional narrative seemed insufficient to describe it. So I watched hours upon hours of Pat Robertson on *The 700 Club,* pretending for the purposes of this book that I held political and religious convictions similar to his (which I don't) while also assuming myself to be a reasonably intelligent and rational person.

The idea was to get to the nexus of Robertson's communications apparatus and judge its merits and powers coolly and objectively, unencumbered by the strong emotions that discussions about basic social and political issues tend to engender. By taking religion out of the equation, I was able to examine Robertson's astoundingly efficient communications machinery.

———<o>———

It just so happens that The Family Channel currently airs reruns of *The Waltons.*

Of course any number of other cable channels could carry this popular 1970s television drama series. All channels run reruns for the same two reasons: They're affordable (especially those that have been in syndication for over a decade) and they're risk-free (assuming they were once successful and remain relatively so).

But the presence of *The Waltons* reruns on the Family Channel is something wholly different. According to Gerard Straub, a producer of *The 700 Club* in the early 1980s, adding reruns of family-oriented television programs to the schedule of the Christian Broadcasting Network (CBN)—the Robertson broadcast entity that spawned the Family Channel and International Family Entertainment—was, at first, simply a way to fill up air time.

Over time and through experimentation, however, Pat Robertson has incorporated these reruns into a radical and breathtaking vision of TV as an effective medium for communicating more than innocuous images.

It was in his 1964 book *Understanding Media: The Extensions of Man* that Marshall McLuhan first identified television as a "cool medium" and therefore more demanding of participation than "hot media," such as print and listening to the radio.

Hot media are "high definition," McLuhan wrote, because they extend a single sense and provide so much information that little room is left for interaction. Cool media—McLuhan included TV, the telephone, and speech in this group—provide a relatively small amount of information and thus require filling-in or completion by the audience.

Literate societies, defined as "hot" by McLuhan, are particularly vulnerable to the disruptive effects of the cool TV medium. Conversely, low-literacy cultures, "cool" societies, in McLuhan's words, "cannot accept hot media like movies or radio entertainment"—that is, they are upset or transformed by them.

Television is generally not thought of as a suitable format for communicating complex or controversial ideas. Print journalists are forever complaining that television obfuscates, rather than elucidates, the motivations of politicians and their potential effectiveness as leaders.

Ronald Reagan is the prime example of an American president who was elected as reward for devising a perfect television image, resolutely cool and low-intensity, rather than for any political ideas his campaign may have engendered. It's no coincidence that Reagan—whose career as a Hollywood actor (remember that movies are "hot" and favor high-intensity performers) was unremarkable—found his greatest success as a politician known for his constant if fuzzy portrayal of a future in which the United States would somewhat resemble the United States of the 1950s.

Nonetheless, Bill Clinton, also presumed to have won the presidency at least in part because of his proficiency as a television personality, seems to have misapprehended the cool medium's particular powers. Unlike Reagan, Clinton acknowledges his cool television image as being separate and apart from his off-screen literate self. Consequently, he is perceived by many Democrats and Republicans alike as indecisive and uncommitted.

Marshall McLuhan in *Understanding Media* quotes Alexis de Tocqueville, nineteenth-century author of *Democracy in America,* responding to the question of why he had not instead written a book about England, another country he respected and was familiar with.

"In America all laws derive in a sense from the same line of thought," De Tocqueville responded, in part. "The whole of society, so to speak, is founded upon a single fact; everything springs from a simple principle. One could compare America to a forest pierced by a multitude of straight roads all converging on the same point. One has only to find the center and everything is revealed at a glance."

It's been a long time since the United States as a whole has possessed the quality of aesthetic integrity that De Tocqueville so admired. But I believe that today the communications empire that Pat Robertson has spent the past thirty years assembling holds a similarly unified aesthetic.

Pat Robertson's principal point has always been, at its core, pretty much the same: The Christian Broadcasting Network, the cornerstone of Robertson's virtual cathedral, states as its official mission (on its Internet site) "to prepare the United States of America, the nations of the Middle East, the Far East, South America, and other nations of the world for the coming of Jesus Christ and the establishment of the kingdom of God on earth. . . . We strive for innovation, excellence, and integrity in all that we do. We aim always to glorify God and His Son Jesus Christ."

It is the "multitude of roads" that converge on that narrow, unbending point that fascinate me.

In that context, an old episode of *The Waltons* being broadcast on the Family Channel is one of those roads.

————◦————

I should state here flatly that finding my way to *The 700 Club* and The Family Channel had absolutely nothing to do with Pat Robertson's message. Suffice it to say that his views on politics and religion, in general, are not mine.

In this book, however, I intend neither to refute nor to endorse the central precepts of Pat Robertson's belief system. Arguments for and against his conservative, sometimes radical politics have been made and are still being made regularly and more knowledgeably elsewhere.

My hunch is that Pat Robertson has been a remarkable success as a broadcaster, organizer, and communicator despite rather than because of his views. In keeping with that hunch, I remain skeptical whether Robertson's strangest, most radical interpretations of history and our culture's present state will ever predicate any noticeable change in the way the average American goes about his or her daily business.

Although 96 percent of Americans say they believe in God or a universal spirit, according to a Gallup poll conducted in December 1994, only 35 percent say they attend religious services on a regular basis and distinguish religion as being "very important" in their lives.

More importantly, of that 35 percent—classified officially by the Gallup Organization as "religious" Americans—only 24 percent said they regarded themselves as members of the religious right movement.

Self-identified members of the religious right movement constitute a mere 8 percent of the American population, according to Gallup.

Assuming that the 96-percent number is inordinately high since those who don't believe in God, or who feel that religion is an especially private matter, aren't likely to participate, the odds seem inordinately slim that any communications engine—even one as powerful and streamlined as Pat Robertson's—will sway additional millions.

Furthermore, recent figures suggest that, despite his much-publicized inroads, Pat Robertson still does not resonate politically, even among Republicans. A New York Times/CBS News poll taken in October 1995 determined that only 13 percent of 478 randomly selected Republican primary voters had a favorable opinion of Robertson; 29 percent had an unfavorable opinion; and 57 percent had no opinion.

In a January 14, 1996, *New York Times Magazine* article titled "The Triumph of Liberalism," Roger Rosenblatt argued that regardless of the countless conservative assaults on the word *liberal* over the past sixteen years, ours remains at essence a liberal nation.

Why, Rosenblatt then wondered, does it appear that liberalism is on the wane? One explanation he matter-of-factly offered was that "public figures who oppose one or another element of liberal thought, like Pat Robertson, Ralph Reed, Pat Buchanan and Newt Gingrich, and right-wing talk-show hosts like G. Gordon Liddy and Rush Limbaugh are more colorful and draw more attention than do their fading targets, like Mario Cuomo or Edward Kennedy."

I would go one step further and argue that Pat Robertson (and by association, his employee-adjunct Ralph Reed)—even more so than the laptop-in-the-lap-of-every-welfare-recipient-minded Gingrich—has made a virtual art out of drawing attention.

It is this art, not the motivations behind it, that is this book's purview.

As I tuned into *The 700 Club* more frequently, I developed an intense curiosity about the avuncular figure who is the show's primary focus (its *secondary* focus, I should say).

In 1988, Pat Robertson went national by running for president. His popularity appeared to peak when he placed an impressive second in that year's Iowa Caucus (Bob Dole came in first; George Bush, third). Although a household name ever since in conservative Christian circles, Pat Robertson occupies a decidedly more Pynchonesque niche in America's secular arena.

Pat Robertson is a quasi celebrity like no other. He is simultaneously everywhere and nowhere. Unless you're a regular viewer of

The 700 Club—broadcast live Monday through Friday from 10 to 11:30 A.M., eastern standard time (and then rebroadcast in an hour-long digest form at 10 P.M. and 2 A.M.), on the Robertson-chaired Family Channel—chances are Pat Robertson is more a familiar name than a familiar face.

"I don't think big-name advertisers look any more kindly upon the Family Channel because of their political bent, and I don't think that anybody looks askance at it because of their political-religious bent," Jon Mandel, a senior vice president at Grey Advertising, told me. "A lot of advertisers really aren't even aware that Pat Robertson chairs the Family Channel."

One look at the Family Channel's 1995–1996 media planner explains why: It contains not a single mention either of Pat Robertson or of God. On the February 1996 program schedule, the time slots ordinarily occupied by *The 700 Club* are instead labeled only "paid programming," an accurate description but a glaring reductio ad absurdum nonetheless.

More recently, opponents have claimed that it is Pat Robertson's mainstream invisibility that makes his presence there such a tremendous threat.

In 1995, the *New York Times*'s Frank Rich authored a series of columns accusing Robertson of pulling political strings from behind the scenes via the Christian Coalition, his grassroots social organization. "Unnoticed by much of the public and unchallenged by much of the press," Rich wrote in one, "a remarkably effective bait-and-switch campaign is now remaking American politics."

Remarkable, indeed. Especially considering that, in addition to building an empire valued at over a quarter billion dollars, Pat Robertson in the course of his career has alternately equated homosexuality with satanism, made plans to televise the Second Coming, and suggested that a worldwide conspiracy engineered by the Trilateral Commission and the Council for Foreign Relations is set to bring to an end both the United States and Christianity.

The same Pat Robertson wrote in his 1991 book *The New World Order,* "Regardless of what anyone may say, America is still a religious nation."

How, I wondered, could a man who subscribed to such oblique

political and religious orthodoxies—old-world fringe theories lost on all but the direst freak doomsayers among us—have traveled this far?

I myself am not enough of a cynic about this country to trust that Robertson's most bizarre utterances are truly a reflection of what a substantive number of Americans believe.

What then has been the real effect of Robertson and his operations on our culture as a whole? Was it conceivable that Pat Robertson's unpopular cant had obscured accomplishments relevant to the secular society that he has spent most of his adult life railing against? Could Robertson's media of expression hold more lasting value than his message?

Remember, for example, that although movable type (the forebear of modern printing) was first invented to disseminate religious literature (Johannes Gutenberg developed the technology in the mid-1400s to print Bibles), one might objectively argue that the medium (printing), not the message (Christianity), has had more widespread influence.

In this spirit I hope to celebrate some of the man's achievements without necessarily celebrating the man.

———◦———

The more I found out about Pat Robertson, the more astounded I was.

As a broadcaster alone, Pat Robertson was one of the medium's great innovators: Robertson started the first Christian television in 1961; he began broadcasting the first Christian talk show, *The 700 Club*, in 1966; in 1971, he became the first Christian satellite operator; when cable television began its rise in the mid-1970s, Robertson was the number three cable operator, right behind Ted Turner and HBO.

Out of *The 700 Club*'s success grew the Christian Broadcasting Network, today a tax-exempt, nonprofit communications engine worth $211.5 million. CBN in turn spawned the $300 million International Family Entertainment, a for-profit public corporation that trades on the New York Stock Exchange. Its holdings include the omnipresent Family Channel, available as part of 98 percent of all basic cable TV packages nationwide.

Then there's Regent University, the 1,500-student graduate-level institution that Robertson founded in 1978 as CBN University to educate like-minded conservative Christians. How many people alive can honestly say they've met someone who has conceived of and subsequently built an accredited private university?

A similar sense of awe should accompany any mention of Pat Robertson's 1988 bid for the Republican presidential nomination. After a surprise second place showing at the Iowa caucuses Robertson's campaign fizzled, but its effects were soon to become historically significant.

And reserve additional huzzahs for the Christian Coalition, the "social activist" organization Robertson established with the mailing lists acquired during his presidential campaign. Today, the Christian Coalition boasts over 1.7 million members across the United States and is considered by many to be the single most powerful political lobbyist group (a claim the coalition itself cannot make, lest it threaten its tax-exempt status).

Stack that alongside accomplishments like the American Center for Law and Justice, a legal advocacy firm started by Robertson that has done the American Civil Liberties Union one better by zealously championing the rights of religious conservatives nationwide—amply bankrolled, of course, by CBN; Operation Blessing, his international missionary effort; and the Founders Inn, a plush Virginia Beach hotel owned by IFE (which Pat Robertson recently tried to spin off into a chain).

"I greatly admire the man for what he's accomplished and his ideas," admitted Skipp Porteous, cofounder of the anti-Robertson Institute for First Amendment Studies, which has painstakingly monitored the radical right movement for nearly a decade. "He's simply brilliant. He's been able to translate his faith into something tangible and find ways through modern technology to reach the world with what he believes. And he is among the first to do that."

In 1994, Jeff Sine of Morgan Stanley's media group made a similar observation. "[Robertson] is viewed as a very smart businessman, along with his son Tim," Sine told *The Washington Post*. "Their results speak for themselves."

"He certainly has to be credited with being one of the visionaries in the business," gushed Fred Dressler, Time Warner Cable's vice president of programming, to *USA Today* in 1992.

Even Ken Auletta, the *New Yorker*'s esteemed media critic, recently hailed Pat Robertson as "both a visionary and a smart businessman."

Here was somebody I wanted to know more about.

———◦———

As I waded deeper into the oceans of available information, I learned something else about Pat Robertson: The guy was extremely difficult to track.

Although he has generated reams of national news coverage over the years, particularly in the last decade, Pat Robertson is a media vampire: When the mainstream media holds up a mirror to him, he gives off no reflection.

This Reverend–Not Reverend (he was once a Baptist minister, but he's not anymore) has made a career of trying to be all things to many people, only never at the same time. To his viewers, he's a grandfatherly sage, meting out Bible-based advice on everything from childrearing to investing. To his advertisers, he's an accomplished business executive, marketing wholesome family programming to the world. To conservative politicians, he's a Republican "peacemaker," as the *Miami Herald*'s Tom Fiedler recently dubbed him, able to lead his flock into whichever paddock the party deems expedient.

And to those who heed him and his ilk, Pat Robertson is a televangelist, the humorously brash TV-age progeny of Elmer Gantry.

Which is the real Pat Robertson?

Of course, they all are. But where is the camera lens wide enough to capture the outer dimensions of this big-league shell game? Which newspaper can spare enough daily column inches to chronicle the worldwide expansionism of a figure many perceive as nothing more than a run-of-the-mill TV preacher? Who has the time or desire to monitor the seven and a half hours a week of live programming that is *The 700 Club*?

Pat Robertson's empire resists summation.

I suspect this Teflon-like quality has as much to do with the American body politic's current state of affairs as much as it does with Robertson's canny ability to gauge it, consistently and accurately.

While conventional politicians and journalists cling to the old labels, liberal and conservative, spender and cutter, Democrat and Republican, unconventional business titans like Robertson are working up whole new categories.

If he existed solely in the secular sector, perhaps he'd be regarded as a conservative Ted Turner, equal parts arrogance and acquisitiveness. Or maybe he would have become a more harshly ideological version of Walt Disney, who, like Robertson, imagined into existence a clean-cut, Anglocentric utopia that, despite its founder's utmost seriousness of purpose, became regarded as high-pop entertainment fluff then turned around and drastically affected America's cultural mainstream in ways its creator could never have dreamed of.

Possibly he would be like Bill Gates, the founder of Microsoft, whose company's knack for envisioning the future software needs of the world's computer users is matched only by its ability to explicate the value of its products to an ever-growing base of customers who only a few years earlier had no need for them.

In some ways Pat Robertson is really the archconservative equivalent of Madonna, the pseudo-outrageous pop icon. Both started out selling an entertainment product (in Madonna's case it was music; in Robertson's, Christian-centered television). Both recognized early on in their careers the potential of using religion as a marketing tool (Madonna commodified her anti-Catholic stance; Robertson, his pan-Christian one). Both maximized their profits and icon potential by feigning victimhood (Madonna as a liberated woman who is persecuted for telling the "truth" about sexuality; Robertson as a liberated freeman who is persecuted for his newfangled religiosity). And both became successful entrepreneurs despite vigorous countertrends within their respective fields of expertise: The heathens believe that meaningful music shouldn't reap limitless profits—and neither should meaningful religion. Robertson wears his point of view like Madonna wears her undergarments—on top of everything else like a suit of armor.

I'm being deliberately irreverent here, but my intent is merely to consider Pat Robertson on the level that he clearly aspires to. Even in the United States, the birthplace of modern fame, few celebrities achieve the sort of mass adulation that lasts more than fifteen minutes. Even fewer reach the pop-culture pantheon, where world famousness retains a whiff of meaning.

That his tenth and latest book, *The End of the Age,* is a light, futuristic novel (his first) that opens with a 300-billion-pound meteor crashing into the Pacific Ocean off the Los Angeles coast is only the most recent evidence that Pat Robertson has learned the true way to the hearts of the American masses. "It's sort of a cross between *Seven Days of May* and *The Omen* as written by someone with the prose style of a Hallmark Cards copywriter," is the way Christopher Buckley characterized the work in *The New York Times Book Review.* Pulp fiction, then, not pulpit oratory, will determine who dominates the attentions of America's booboisie in the twenty-first century. Give Robertson credit for reading the signs of the times.

In a February 1996 issue of *Time* magazine, Nicholas Lemann codified three distinct paths to success that compete with each other in the United States: talent, lifer, and mandarin.

"Talents" are America's traditional self-starters, Lemann wrote, individuals who got where they are based on taking big risks in unstructured environments (entrepreneurs and performers fall into this category); "lifers" are those who join large corporations or bureaucracies and work their way up through the ranks; and "mandarins" are the intelligent, overeducated elite (university presidents, foundation heads, and Wall Street types fit in this category).

Lemann identified Bob Dole and "most corporate CEOs" as lifers, Pat Buchanan and Ronald Reagan as talents, and Bill Clinton as a mandarin.

While Lemann's labeling was admittedly somewhat arbitrary, it helped make a valid point about the forces that continue to cleave American society. What was most striking to me, however, was how smashingly Pat Robertson stacked up as product of each of the three paths.

Pat Robertson is by all means a "talent": Having founded a successful corporation, a university, and a powerful lobbying organization, all while earning himself a fair modicum of fame would seem to instantly qualify him here. But he's a "mandarin," too: He was raised to be a member of what Lemann called the Episcopacy, the ruling gentlemen class that historically preceded the mandarins; and, after all, where would he be without his Yale Law education, his strong ties to the Washington establishment, and his big, morality-bound ideas? Finally, Pat Robertson is, of course, the ultimate "lifer," having dedicated his every last breath to climbing the ranks of Christendom.

All of this is just another way of saying that Pat Robertson has always pursued his will in every possible way within his means.

———◇———

To understand today's most technically evolved methods of communications is to avoid falling prey to their persuasive powers. Pat Robertson has been labeled by his foes as a televangelist, a cult leader, and a theocrat. These labels are irrelevant because they diminish Robertson and dismiss his influence beyond his flock.

This book is not about religion. I believe the story of the other Pat Robertson, the one that built a better mousetrap, will outlast any perfunctory perspective he may bring to his faith.

What this book is, is an effort to track Robertson's influence beyond his own self-definition. For any mogul worth his or her salt, this ought to be the highest of honors.

"The successor to politics will be propaganda," Marshall McLuhan once predicted. "Propaganda, not in the sense of a message or ideology, but as the impact of the whole technology of the times." I'm convinced Pat Robertson is a propagandist in this exteroceptive sense of the word.

As you read through the following pages, pay attention not to what Pat Robertson is saying but how he says it and you too will discover what I have: In these times of techno-prompted democratization, communications innovation can emerge from the unlikeliest of quarters. And that giving that innovation its due is the surest way to defuse a powder keg of radical destructive thought.

CHAPTER TWO

---◆---

Monday Morning, 10:00 A.M.

D o you value, as I do, your right to have your voice heard in
Washington about the issues that affect your family?" That's Pat
Robertson on *The 700 Club*. "Well, the Congress doesn't seem to
think so." Robertson looks radiant during this, his first television
broadcast of one week in October 1994. Dapper in an elegant navy
suit, a tasteful red-print tie, a scarlet handkerchief peeking out of his
breast pocket, he doesn't raise his voice when he directs this perfectly
reasonable observation to the television camera. His words dance in
even, sonorous tones up and down a narrow musical scale, his lips
pursed in practiced embouchure, like an oboist masterfully exhaling
his way through a Handel concerto. —*Well, the Congress doesn't seem
to think so*— He's well-mannered and dignified, the way Ronald Reagan was at his peak—he's even wearing one of those wonderful, full-
cut white shirts that Reagan always wore, with the floppy, napkin-size
collars meant to partially conceal a smooth, prosperous jowl. His fair,
sandy-gray hair is carefully combed, but not overly stiffened like most
newscasters. His breeding comes across, even on TV. On the wall
behind Robertson is a map of the world, the magically luminescent
kind—an earth-tone geographic mass hovering over a bright ocean-
blue background—that sits behind virtually every news anchor
nationwide at the start of the evening news. So, it's no surprise when,
minutes into *The 700 Club,* a video display swings into the upper-
right-hand corner of the screen, and Robertson launches into a digest
of the day's events. First, it's the situation in Haiti. "America takes its
first serious 'casualty' in its occupation of Haiti," Robertson says.

Apparently, an Army special-forces member, who remains unnamed, was shot at midnight by an unidentified Haitian. Before he can give any further details, a news clip rolls. Over footage of a young black man running down a dirt road shooting a rifle, Paul Strand of CBN (the Christian Broadcasting Network)—explains in a voice-over that 1800 Marines are pulling out of Haiti, to be replaced by 300 "peace-keepers from Caribbean nations." Republican congressman Newt Gingrich and Senator John Warner ("the top Republican on the Senate Armed Services committee") are paraphrased; they both want American troops out of Haiti as quickly as possible. The video coverage from Haiti could easily run on CNN (Ted Turner's Cable News Network) or CBS's *60 Minutes*. There's even a little CBN News identification logo hovering in the lower-right-hand corner of the screen. It makes things look sharp, *professional.* The video clips run silent, except for incidental noise like gunshots and shouts, as the commentator reads his copy. File shots of Gingrich, Warner, the Capitol building and exiled Haitian president Jean-Bertrand Aristide flash amid the generic combat footage. Sure, these random portrayals of violence could have been sluiced from any number of war sites, past or present. But they appear credible, and there is no reason to believe they are not: The collage techniques by which today's television news programs tell the stories of the day were long ago perfected. Truth is too subjective a term; credibility *is* the truth. And CBN News's Haiti update so far seems—if not particularly detailed; remember, it's TV—perfectly credible, perfectly *reasonable.* . . .

————◦————

. . . "All I can say is, Thank the Lord this was not a *fatal* injury to this American," says Terry Meeuwsen, Robertson's perky cohost, after the news clip ends. (It wasn't fatal? Robertson called it a "casualty.") Sitting at Robertson's right, dressed in a smart canary yellow suit with black trim, Meeuwsen looks a lot like *Entertainment Tonight*'s Mary Hart. (In fact, she was Miss America 1973.) The broad smile, the healthy glow, and the frosted, helmet hairdo might bespeak superficiality in the real world, but in Television Land they connote homespun believability. When Robertson expresses his concern for the way the mayhem reflects on President Clinton's reputation ("They should have sent a peace mission—a high-level mission—about a year ago") he comes off as a voice of moderation. (Is not peaceful conciliation always preferable to combat?) Then Meeuwsen launches into the story behind the story: Jean-Bertrand Aristide. Aristide, she tells Robertson—"the man the United States is being asked to restore to power in Haiti"— may have received funding from the Colombian Medellín drug cartel. Meeuwsen certainly seems to be well-informed about the crisis. But as she takes a breath between sentences, Meeuwsen gracefully swivels toward the camera. No longer is she conversing with Robertson—she's now issuing her own news brief. The video display drifts back into place, this time in the upper-left-hand corner of the screen. Meeuwsen repeats the details of a story attributed to the *Washington Times,* the decidedly conservative newspaper owned by Sun Myung Moon's Unification Church (which even Robertson has labeled a "cult"), that has recently gained enough respect for its reporters to appear as right-wingers on C-SPAN and CNN. And the details are savory, succulent morsels. Allegedly, a suitcase stuffed with cash was handed to Aristide back in 1991 in return for safe passage of cocaine through Haiti. If the story is a true one, it's a terrific detail. It's hard to say for sure whether or not it is—but if it were, then this is exactly the kind of stuff I would want to know. And maybe it's not as outlandish as it seems. The *Washington Times* isn't the only paper that has questioned Aristide's integrity; last year, more liberal news organizations—namely, the *Nation* and the *New York Times*—reported that CIA-funded informants in the Haitian government had turned to political violence and drug-running. Furthermore, according to a front-page *New York Times* article dated October 8, 1994, the Drug Enforcement Administration (DEA) intended to investigate Father Aristide's connection to Colombian drug dealers until a review committee decided that the details of the sole informant's account didn't check out. "Can you imagine an American dying for that guy?" mutters a mildly ruffled Robertson. (Well, the guy's not actually dead; but it *could* happen.) And Robertson knows even more: "Unofficial" intelligence sources, he says, report that Fidel Castro is shutting down Cuba's drug-trafficking channels in an effort to curry favor with the U.S. administration— therefore, drug lords have been eyeing Haiti as a new connecting port.

———◁○▷———

Television was invented for this. On TV, everything is in the present tense. Fast-paced images, slick cuts, news updates from around the world, genial hosts, celebrity guests, detailed analyses of the day's events—if only MTV were this good, this effective. How did Robertson get here? Where else is he? I'm part of the secular world that Pat Robertson gently counsels against in his mannered and cultured tones. I suspect most Americans are. But somehow Robertson gets to me. For some reason my thumb's touch lightens up on the channel changer's button whenever Pat Robertson's generous smile flickers on-screen. In the following pages, you'll learn about Robertson's past; and every few chapters, you'll tune into his present. Technological breakthroughs have made the latest in television graphics available to virtually any media outlet, big or small. And the software is evolving as quickly as the hardware. Most television amounts to opinionless chatter—Robertson has changed the rules by giving television a direction and purpose. He is history and the future acting as one cybernetic organism.

———◁○▷———

Now it's a smooth transition into a video bit on the Lobbying Disclosure Act pending in Congress. According to Robertson's report, it's nothing more than a "gag rule" being proposed by legislators to silence grassroots lobbyists. "The people in Congress, the liberals, are doing things we don't like," he carefully explains, "but they don't want to listen any longer to the voice of the people. They don't want you and me to talk about it." This time a video montage with voice-over is bolstered by a following discussion that Robertson has with conservative pundit Gary Bauer, whom he describes as a former adviser to the president (Reagan, that is) and now the president of the Family Research Council, a "pro-family public policy organization." Bauer is in Washington, which allows CBN to show off its impressive split-screen technology. It's clear that Bauer is in Washington because he's got one of those Capitol building backdrops behind him that's no different from the kind that even the tony *MacNeil NewsHour* uses to denote place. What's most shocking about all this stuff is not the political platform that Robertson is setting forth. Robertson's opinions are probably exactly what you would expect, whether or not you agree with them. What's most arresting is how natural all of this feels. Conventional wisdom dictates that people like Pat Robertson are hucksters. That so-called mainstream news sources—objective sources—are more reliable. But Robertson is no huckster in the classic sense—if anything, he's reassuringly up-front about where he stands on each and every issue he discusses. His details often check out. After the exchange with Gary Bauer, Robertson recommends that viewers call the Senate if they want to alert their legislators. He flashes the Senate address and phone number on the screen. "It's called S349, the Lobby Reform and Disclosure Act," he says. . . .

——◄○►——

Now comes the self-promotion portion of the show. For a $31 contribution to *The 700 Club,* you get a six-month subscription to the *Fact Sheet File,* an issues newsletter. Terry Meeuwsen then reports on a conference held at Regent University, the institution of higher learning founded by the Christian Broadcasting Network. A debate on the separation of church and state, moderated by former *New Republic* and current *Roll Call* editor Morton Kondracke, featured "both liberals and conservatives." Most of the panelists, in truth, are conservative, like nationally syndicated columnist Don Feder and soon-to-be presidential hopeful Dr. Alan Keyes, although the presence of the Reverend Barry Lynn of Americans United for the Separation of Church and State is a notable exception who provides a convincing opposing viewpoint. The panelist who gets the most air time in this segment, however, is Jay Sekulow of the American Center for Law and Justice, the conservative legal organization that Robertson formed on the model of the American Civil Liberties Union. Pat Robertson didn't invent this kind of intraorganizational logrolling. These days, it's not unusual for the major networks to make the debut of a new sitcom a "story" on the evening news. During the Haitian crisis, Dan

Rather showed up, inexplicably, on CBS's *Entertainment Tonight* to assure viewers that everything was going smoothly. Most television stations are now owned by international multimedia conglomerates that also own movie studios, recording labels, and publishers—cross-promotion has become the rule, not the exception. But Pat Robertson nearly invented this stuff in the 1970s. "Well, the Supreme Court begins its new term today," Robertson says. "And one of the things before the learned justices is, Does the Bible you find in your motel room need a warning label?" This is Robertson's introduction to another round of news briefs from Richard Hunt, another CBN talking head: The Supreme Court is beginning its 1994–1995 session by weighing in on term limits for legislators; Bill Clinton offered a last-minute settlement offer to Paula Jones, the woman who first publicly declared on *The 700 Club* that he sexually harassed her; a group called the Freedom From Religion Foundation is slapping stickers on Gideon Bibles in hotel rooms that "warn people about the dangers of reading scripture." So Robertson got his facts a little confused—the Supreme Court isn't actually considering whether or not to ban Bibles, after all. But at least the real facts were in there somewhere. He corrects himself later on. During the next segment, Robertson answers personal finance questions from the studio audience. The first questioner inquires as to the financial toll that government welfare programs wreaks on the average consumer. (No surprise: Aren't most television audience participants fed questions?) The other two participants request basic investing information. The show's pacing is quick; impressive computer graphics are used whenever possible. After another plug for the *Fact Sheet File*, Robertson and Meeuwsen return. Now they're seated in a living-room set much like the ones featured on network morning shows such as *Good Morning America* and *Today*. Call the 24-hour prayer line. A tour of Regent University's brand-new accredited law school. Former vice president Dan Quayle shows his support. Operation Blessing, Robertson's poverty outreach program, has a new Lockheed jet. Lawyers have a moral responsibility to their profession. An hour later, you've been given a point of view and a perspective on a healthy variety of the day's issues, plus a positive vibe and the knowledge that Robertson is riding the zeitgeist, the fast lane of the information highway.

Now we're watching a tape made at the "grand finale" dinner at a weekend dedication of Regent University's graduate center. It begins with Nancy Stainback singing a piercing, operatic rendition of "America, the Beautiful." Except that she begins with the anthem's obscure fourth verse, which goes, "O beautiful for patriot dream / That sees beyond the years, / Thine alabaster cities gleam, / Undimmed by human tears." After the final "God shed His grace on thee, / And crown thy good with brotherhood / From sea to shining sea" she adds a drawn-out "*A-a-a-men.*" It's a brilliant juxtaposition that's reaffirmed in the tuxedo-clad Robertson's subsequent comments. "I realize that you and I are sitting in a room that is only eleven miles away from the place where the first English-speaking settlers came to the United States of America," he says. The date was April 26, 1607. Robertson's account of the establishment of the Jamestown colony reminds that, upon arriving, the settlers carried a "seven-foot oak cross" from one of the ships and placed it in the ground and prayed. The confluence of fact and fulmination is an astute one. Robertson's characterization of the settlers' "burning desire to establish a just government based on the principles of the Bible" seems reasonably accurate. The spin comes when he goes on to lambaste everyone from the Supreme Court to the "institutions of power" for outright betraying the original intentions of the Founding Fathers. Stainback's back with a cloying version of "God Bless America" (poor Irving Berlin). Fireworks. Now Cheryl Prewitt Salem, Miss America 1980 is being interviewed. She's got a bright, toothy smile, a slight Mississippi drawl, and an elegant bunch of pearl necklaces dangling from her neck. She says that she knew she was going to win the Miss America Pageant because the Lord came to her at the age of seventeen and told her she was destined to win. "And that was really hard for the press that year," she says. And did you know that Prewitt was the last Miss America to be crowned by Burt Parks? That's what she says. She also reveals that she was in a car accident at age eleven that left her crippled for six years. She seems chatty, relaxed, articulate. Meeuwsen presses further: "Tell us about what happened to you as a child." Prewitt then confesses to Meeuwsen that she was sexually molested as a youth. "When I first started dealing with this issue," she says, "I told the Lord, I will do this, I'm allowing you to heal me, and I'll take this healing to other people, if you'll promise me that you'll keep this out of the national media." God as the ultimate press liaison is as apt a metaphor for the scope of Pat Robertson's vision as any; and Oprah Winfrey would be proud. An hour later, after a few minutes of healing prayers, this morning's *700 Club* broadcast is over. News, information, guidance, entertainment, three times a day, five days a week. I'm telling you, this Robertson guy? He's a *genius.*

———◁◦▷———

Now it's over a year later. Christmas season 1995. December 29, to be precise, and we're watching the end of the last *700 Club* broadcast of the year. Here are Pat Robertson, Terry Meeuwsen, and Ben Kinchlow, the lanky African-American with white hair and a cotton-ball mustache who has played Ed McMahon to Robertson's Johnny Carson for most years since 1977. They're sitting in cloth-covered armchairs on a bright morning-show set (wintry trees through French doors) in front of a giant Christmas tree. One minute ago, everyone was all smiles and chit-chat. But now they're holding hands, their eyes scrunched shut in prayer. "Now, there's somebody who has an impacted wisdom tooth—God is healing that situation right now," begins Robertson, who is presumably addressing someone who is not present. "—In the name of Jesus, there's somebody else who has an infection of the sinuses and the Lord is healing as we speak." Frankly, this is just the kind of behavior that has kept Pat Robertson from being hailed as a space-age synergist. "Words of knowledge," the Pentecostal Christian practice of faith-healing we're watching here, doesn't strike most people as appropriate behavior for a media mogul. But Pat Robertson is no ordinary televangelist, either. The term "televangelist" conjures up crude backwater preachers like Jerry Falwell, Jimmy Swaggart, Oral Roberts, and Jim Bakker. Robertson is different. Marion G. "Pat" Robertson—born March 22, 1930—stands alone. The son of a distinguished United States senator, the descendant of two presidents, Robertson was born into greatness. In 1988, he even tried running for president himself. "Somebody else has a problem with drainage in the ear, the Eustachian tubes have been blocked and so forth," he continues. "God is healing you right now, even as we're speaking. In Jesus's name, somebody has a great problem with phlegm—you're coughing phlegm—God is healing your lungs and your throat right now. In the name of Jesus, all infection shall leave you. Cancer is being taken away, someone with leukemia, there's a little child that's got leukemia—God is healing that child. Mercy, in Jesus' name. Thank you, Lord. There's a stomach problem, a duodenal ulcer is being healed, an adominable, uh, abdominal ulcer is being healed. Somebody else has ulcerating colitis, they're being healed right now by the power of God. Just this heat going into your body, even as we speak." In 1981, the Christian Broadcasting Network began accepting commercial advertising, thus planting the seed that grew into today's International Family Entertainment, the successful public corporation chaired by Robertson which posted sales totaling nearly $300 million in 1995. It's Terry Meeuwsen's turn: "You have cancer of the stomach and it's been diagnosed," she says, "and God is healing that for you and you'll feel that warmth and, almost a feeling of warm oil flowing through your stomach." And the tax-exempt Christian Broadcasting Network continues on, with revenues in excess of $211 million, including over $90 million in donations. "I confirm that word," Ben Kinchlow rejoins, "and someone else has, I'm not sure it's cancer but you have a problem with your liver and God's healing that, because whatever that problem is with your liver, God is healing it now. And there's someone else that has problems with your upper intestine and then maybe the same person but there's a blockage in lower intestine—God's healing that in Jesus's name." Running for president, commandeering the most powerful political organization in the country, founding a university, establishing an international brand name in family entertainment rivaled only by Disney—Pat Robertson has done it all. But right now, he's got a holiday message for you: "Somebody, the only way I can describe it is that your lungs are just rotten, you're literally coughing up bits of your lung tissue, and I don't know what it is, it's not emphysema, but it could have been some kind of a fungus that's come and gone. God is healing you completely. COMPLETELY! You can cough and everything's coming up and then you can breathe and from then on your lungs are healed. By the power of God, someone has got a terrible problem right in the center of your skull, I don't know what that is, it's just anguish, anguish, and God is healing it. Every bit of the problem is leaving right now. Ben, you have another one." A dollar donated to *The 700 Club* has never been simply a matter of "pleasing God," as the show's direct-mail literature phrases it. It's been so much more. "I don't know exactly what this is," says Kinchlow, "but it's like a very peculiar checkered square floor, the floor is very peculiar and it's a design, and you are praying specifically about a problem and God is going to answer positively in that matter, and you know it's you because of the design of that floor. God's gonna heal that." Robertson's empire is a little bit like that unusually patterned floor, dizzying and hard to describe. The odds are pretty good you've come in contact with it, either consciously or unconsciously. But to grasp the full extent of it would be something akin to trying to absorb every minute of every channel on television in one night. "Now there's somebody who's praying for $45,000," Robertson is saying, as he raises his left palm up to the screen, "and you basically told God if he doesn't supply your needs you're just going to die, you're going to kill yourself, you just can't stand life anymore. God's going to supply your need, and don't ever think those thoughts. God is setting you free, you don't have to do something for money, you live for Him and praise Him, and He'll take care of your need, in the name of Jesus." This is the story of how a secular man of exceptional talent and poise used his religious faith to gild a much grander vision. Could Pat Robertson be corporate America's approximation of poet Ezra Pound, a brilliant but embattled intellect, or is he merely a man who has adopted other's innovations for his own otherworldly device? "And while we're praying, Lord, we pray for our country," Robertson says in conclusion, "we pray for our government, we pray for the Congress and the President. We pray, oh Lord, for the leadership: God Almighty, give us righteous leaders in America, we pray. And as we end this year we thank you for all the blessing you bestowed on us, and we thank you for what you're going to do in the year to come. We praise you, our Father, in Jesus's name. Amen."

CHAPTER THREE

The Empire

P at Robertson was enthralled. The flamed-shaped cake, iced bright orange with jelly, looked big enough to feed fifty. Gathered round him and the mammoth pastry were eight men, all in business suits, and one woman, here to celebrate the sixty-fifth birthday of the man who had first drawn them together. It was the morning of March 23, 1995, and everything was going Pat Robertson's way.

"This is a beautiful birthday!" Robertson exhorted, squinting his twinkly eyes with a smile. "We're so glad to have everyone here."

And, indeed, everyone was.

To his right were Bob Fanning of Operation Blessing and Ralph Reed of the Christian Coalition. Beside them, John Damoose of International Family Entertainment; Keith Fournier of the American Center for Law and Justice; Terry Lindvall of Regent University; and Michael Little and Bob Slosser of the Christian Broadcasting Network.

There to do the honors and cut the cake was Ben Kinchlow, Robertson's trusty sidekick. The silver-haired woman, dripping in elegant pearl brocade, was Dede Robertson, a CBN board member and the boss's wife for over 40 years.

Celebrity well-wishers like Kathie Lee Gifford and Gavin McLeod had showered the legendary broadcaster birthday greetings via prerecorded video. Republican presidential hopeful Bob Dole delivered his video greeting with rare comedic timing: "I hope you and Dede can celebrate your sixty-seventh birthday in the White House—with Bob and Elizabeth Dole."

And let's not forget the studio audience and million-plus viewers of *The 700 Club,* who witnessed this morning's events, as always, live on the air.

In the three and a half decades since Pat Robertson had kindled his business with a three-dollar bank deposit, much had changed. Having devoted nearly a lifetime to combating bigotry against what he called the world's most persecuted minority, fundamentalist Christians, he had every right to claim victory. That this historic gathering took place live on the air, in Robertson's own high-tech television studio, made the occasion all the more distinguished. With the overflow of contributions CBN supporters had mailed in over the years "to change the world," Pat Robertson had erected a virtual cathedral, whose diverse elements were worth some half a billion dollars combined.

No doubt longtime *700 Club* donors were already aware that their hard-earned pledges fed into a nonprofit web of Christian social services. Over the past three decades, Robertson had assembled a phalanx of social support organizations, among them the Operation Blessing missionary effort, the all-graduate Regent University, and the American Center for Law and Justice legal defense group, all devoted to "sharing God's love," as he had phrased it in one fundraising letter.

Perhaps fewer, though, had stepped back and gazed upon the larger picture, the one that framed Robertson as the multimillionaire chairman of International Family Entertainment, a healthy public corporation (revenues up 12 percent in 1995), and political kingmaker. Those who had were no doubt even more impressed.

"This is not what one man has done, this is what God has done through one man" is how Ben Kinchlow put it moments later on the Virginia Beach soundstage, as those assembled joined hands and bowed their heads in prayer under the harsh glare of the studio klieg lights.

Providence had truly smiled on Pat Robertson.

———<o>———

Things hadn't always been this way. Had *700 Club* viewers tuned in to their favorite morning-TV personality's program in 1988, they would have found the Christian talk show host wading through waves of organizational static.

The handsome profits generated by Robertson's CBN Satellite Network, recently renamed The Family Channel, were jeopardizing his nonprofit status.

An importunately timed series of well-publicized televangelist scandals, including Oral Roberts's plea for funds to head off his death, Jim Bakker's adulterous affair and fraudulent business practices, and Jimmy Swaggart's teary on-air admission of relations with prostitutes, had left the American public's appetite for religious broadcasters in a slump.

Having recently waged and lost a bid for the Republican presidential nomination while ratings for his beloved *700 Club* plummeted in his absence, Robertson was left to return home and confront his encroaching financial woes.

Not that Robertson was a novice when it came to corporate wheeling and dealing. If anything, he prided himself on having always been a leader—nay, a martyr—in the field of marshaling funds in the name of Jesus Christ.

As far as the former Golden Gloves middleweight was concerned, his string of bouts with agencies like the Internal Revenue Service (IRS) and the Securities and Exchange Commission (SEC) were merely emblems of his enduring struggle.

Robertson had locked horns with tax-collecting authorities as early as 1971, when the city of Portsmouth, Virginia, the troubled metropolis where his network began, tried to collect back taxes it claimed CBN owed for 1969 and 1970. "Deeply concerned" by the city's reclassification of CBN's holdings, CBN initiated a suit against the city to "determine our status in this regard."

Robertson subsequently made local headlines when he acknowledged Portsmouth's financial difficulties, dismissed the suit, and delivered a check for $50,000—double the amount due—along with a letter to the town's mayor explaining the twofold repayment was "what the Lord wanted us to do."

In 1974, the SEC filed a civil suit against CBN for its failure to disclose a "deteriorating financial condition" to investors in 27 states who had purchased $7.3 million in interest-bearing notes. Although Robertson admitted to no wrongdoing, CBN agreed to upgrade its financial disclosure to avoid drawn-out litigation.

But this time was different. At stake was the future of Robertson's whole enterprise, by now a microkingdom which only a few years earlier claimed annual revenues approaching $200 million, with contributions totaling $135 million.

At stake was his reputation, brought into question (some said unfairly) by other's misdeeds; and his honor, besmirched during his campaign by those who accused him of, among other misdeeds, falsifying the details of his résumé and Korean War record.

In business, Robertson had long been buoyed by his strategic edge. After all, this was the guy who was third in line—just behind Home Box Office and Turner Broadcasting System—when RCA catapulted its revolutionary SacCom 1 communications satellite into orbit in 1975.

On April 29, 1977, CBN switched on its earth station and became the first religious broadcaster with a full-time transponder. The new satellite technology enabled networks to deliver programming to local affiliates equipped with dish antennas via microwave transmissions at a relatively low cost.

Well-positioned for the latest developments in television, CBN became the country's first channel to offer 24-hour "basic service," or free signal reception, to cable subscribers.

By 1988, Robertson's network, now called CBN Family Channel, was available to 41.6 million subscribers on 8,215 affiliates. (For purposes of comparison, the ESPN sports channel, then the most popular cable network, reached 47.8 million subscribers through 9,500 affiliates.)

Flying high, CBN Family Channel was the eighth largest cable network, right up there with brand names like CNN, MTV, and the USA Network.

———◆———

The trouble really started back in 1986 with a particular missive Pat Robertson dispatched to his supporters.

"The Christians have won!" trumpeted a jubilant Robertson in the correspondence dated June 19, referring to the fruitful delegate-registration drive in Michigan. "Our work was most dramatically demonstrated," Robertson wrote, "by the fact that, on the Republican side of the response, the delegate applicants that we educated, trained, and motivated outnumbered the delegate applicants registered through the efforts of both Vice President George Bush and United States Congressman Jack Kemp."

Robertson proceeded to wow fellow Republicans by roping a respectable plurality in Michigan's August 1986 precinct caucuses.

Unfortunately, the letter was printed on stationery from the Freedom Council, a nonprofit organization Robertson hatched in 1981 "to help defend, restore and preserve religious freedom in the United States," as one brochure stated.

The Freedom Council had been granted provisional tax-exempt status only a month earlier under section 501(c)(3) of the Internal Revenue code.

By October Pat Robertson had pledged to run for president on the Republican ticket if three million registered voters signed petitions within a year.

By choosing to run for the highest elected office in the land, Robertson willingly subjected himself and his organizations to a level of financial scrutiny, as well as a gargantuan media shitstorm, the likes of which they had never before weathered.

In the weeks after Robertson officially declared his candidacy in October 1987, Michael J. McManus, writing in his syndicated column Ethics & Religion, broke the news that the Christian Broadcasting Network had heaped $8.5 million into Freedom Council accounts in preparation for the campaign.

CBN's tax returns, public record by law, showed that the organization had loaned $821,000 to the Freedom Council in the period ending March 1985 and $939,000 in the period ending March 1986. Neither loan had been repaid. Columnist McManus later reported that CBN had sent an estimated $3 million the Freedom Council's way in the period leading up to Robertson's declaration. Add another $3.7 million that CBN donated to the National Freedom Institute, a Freedom Council precursor, and the picture was clear.

Although Robertson continued to argue that having a hand in various and distinct corners of the public square merely bore testament to his faith and that charges of political profligacy were prejudicial, example after example rendered the argument more improbable.

Operation Blessing, an outreach program founded by Robertson, gave over $200,000 in aid to failing farmers in Iowa during 1986. Was it ever fair to question such beneficence, even upon discovering that the giving in Iowa—home to an early, influential presidential caucus— amounted to ten times more than Robertson had sent the way of any other troubled Midwestern farm state?

Robertson himself admitted that Operation Blessing, the kind of missionary effort for which a Christian ministry ostensibly raises funds, operated with minimal overhead. "We just allocate money from our general revenue and we take that into an inner city," he said, "and we tell a church there 'If you are really concerned about helping your people we will match what you give.' We go to a private business and say 'If you've got some surplus rice, beans, or flour we will facilitate the transportation and distribution.' So we call that *leveraged* things."

That CBN/Operation Blessing happened to have "leveraged" $2 million in Operation Blessing funds in the mid-1980s to refugee camps run by the Contras in Honduras with the help of Friends of the Americas and the Air Commandos Association, two American groups distinguished by their charity toward anti-Sandinista activities, could be attributed to aiding the victims of Communist menace, much in the fashion of the Reagan Administration.

In September 1986, Robertson disbanded the Freedom Council in a move some speculated was a heartfelt attempt on the candidate's part to abide by complicated tax and election laws. The IRS had already initiated an audit of the financial arrangements between CBN and its affiliated organizations.

Either way Robertson's political activities were hindering the flow of donations at CBN, according to the *Roanoke Times & World-News*. In 1985, CBN's annual January telethon yielded an all-time high of around $75 million; in 1986, the year Robertson informally announced his candidacy, contributions dropped to under $50 million; in 1987, the same telethon grossed a paltry $33 million.

Time devoted to his presidential run took away from time Robertson would have spent otherwise tending to CBN. In 1987, Robertson's 32-year-old son Timothy took over as president of the network.

More debilitating was Tim Robertson's takeover of his father's cohost spot on *The 700 Club*. The junior Robertson, who had a reputation for being substantially less petulant than Dad offscreen, came off dull and wooden in front of the camera, despite a passing resemblance to his predecessor. In his stead, *The 700 Club*'s typically conservative viewpoint came off as even more strident. Each time Tim Robertson sputtered his way through another TelePrompTer-fed rant, he issued an unintentional tribute to his father's soothing, seamless performance.

Between 1986 and 1988, CBN's viewership plunged somewhere between 30 to 50 percent. Forced to downsize, CBN sliced its budget by $34 million and sacked 645 employees.

Although Pat Robertson placed a surprise second in the Iowa GOP caucuses of 1988, his presidential bid landed with a resounding thud when he sank to fourth on Super Tuesday.

By July Robertson was writing his supporters, begging for their sympathies ("The price was brutal. There was physical exhaustion. My faith was ridiculed. My motives and words were distorted. Lies were spread about my war record, my education and my résumé. My family was savagely wounded. . . .") and for their enduring financial support ("The future is very encouraging if we can close down the 1988 campaign debt-free. Your gift of $25 is crucial to pay off the last $990,000 remaining. . . .").

Adding insult to injury, the Federal Election Commission fined Robertson $25,000 for breaking a law that prohibited presidential hopefuls from declaring themselves as candidates (so defined by spending over $5,000 seeking a nomination). On September 17, 1986, Robertson had blown more than $4 million to fly a closed-circuit broadcast of an Americans for Robertson rally, live from Constitution Hall in Washington.

By May 1988, Americans for Robertson had spent over $20 million to fund a presidential campaign that garnered the candidate a total of 17 state delegates. Waterlogged by debt and unfairly cowed, he said, by the media, Robertson retreated to Virginia Beach to regroup.

In August 1989, CBN Family Channel became simply The Family Channel, a change made to assuage the IRS (which objects to tax-exempt organizations that attribute more than 50 percent of their revenues from commercial activities) and Robertson's oblique way of suggesting that religion needed to take a back seat to profits if there were any hope of sustaining the whole operation. Unlike its predecessor, The Family Channel would generate its own profits, independent of CBN.

By recasting his network as a preserve of G-rated, family entertainment Pat Robertson was able to make commercial hay off a unique brand of television counterprogramming that he had pioneered out of necessity when CBN Satellite Network first began accepting advertisements in the early 1980s.

Sidled with three to four and a half hours of the low-rated *The 700 Club* in its prime-time slots, CBN had always sought to draw large audiences at unusual hours. In the mid-eighties, the network loaded up its late-night roster with classic TV comedies like *Burns and Allen, Dobie Gillis,* and *The Very Best of Groucho* for those viewers weary of the evening news and talk shows aired by most channels in that time slot. On Saturday and Sunday afternoons, CBN showed Western reruns like *Wagon Train, The Virginian,* and *Gunsmoke* and drew an adult-male audience 50 percent larger than the cable sports channel ESPN.

In order to withstand the brave new world of financial independence, The Family Channel needed a new broadcasting philosophy plus original programming to grow a brand name. This time uncomplicated religious hybrids of the sort CBN had kited on a shoestring in the mid-1980s—like *Another Life,* a Christian soap opera, and *USa.m.,* a morning talk program with religious overtones—just wouldn't do.

Since 1988, CBN had sought an outside buyer for The Family Channel. But the criteria for purchase were stiff: CBN demanded fair market value with a potentially unmarketable twist. The buyer would not only have to guarantee that The Family Channel would remain a family-oriented basic cable station but also agree to block out choice chunks of the prime-time schedule to air *The 700 Club* ad infinitum and share the proceeds of any future appreciation with CBN. To boot, The Family Channel sought the elimination of $46.4 million in liabilities incurred by CBN's film library. In short, Pat Robertson wanted to have his giant flame-shaped cake and eat it, too.

Although Robertson reportedly harbored secret hopes that a solution could be found within, the services of Communications Equity Associates, a cable investment banker, were retained to search for potential buyers. In the months ahead, none emerged.

Enter John C. Malone, the notoriously inviolable head of the Denver-based Tele-Communications Inc., the country's largest cable operator. In Malone, Robertson found the architect for future plans grander than he could have possibly imagined.

By tailoring the whole programming schedule to its stringently blinkered view of the world, The Family Channel had inadvertently scooped an early-1990s media trend toward wholesome entertainment. "Family products are 'in,' " Robertson later observed in his 1993 book *The Turning Tide*. "Today's film powerhouses—Lucas, Spielberg, Disney—all cater to family audiences, and they make hundreds of millions of dollars in the process. . . . Now that such remarkable success is being achieved with computerized special effects, digital animation, and live-action animation, I see a proliferation of this film form that lends itself so readily to clean family programs."

John Malone, who initiated negotiations with Robertson behind closed doors, agreed. "Pat Robertson's church was faced with having to sell that channel," Malone later told the Senate Judiciary Committee during an antitrust hearing, "which we thought was valuable to a large section of our subscribers, because it's a family-oriented, good-quality service. It has a particular niche audience."

Malone's TCI spent the eighties borrowing money and buying up nearly 90 percent of the cable properties that came on the market at prices other cable operators considered overvalued. Respected more for assessing balance sheets than appraising program quality, Malone saw the Pat Robertson others had missed—Pat Robertson, the savvy businessman.

While the CBN ministry hobbled along, the Family Channel had emerged as 1989's second-fastest-growing cable network in advertising sales. Seventy percent of its revenues came from commercials; the other 30 from cable companies, which paid The Family Channel 8 cents per month per subscriber (only four years earlier, CBN bucked the norm by paying the *operators* 20 cents per subscriber!).

Robertson had also nipped back religious programming to less than 25 percent of the schedule. In the second quarter of 1989, the five highest-rated programs on The Family Channel were all westerns: *Bonanza, Gunsmoke, The Rifleman, Wagon Train,* and *Bordertown.* They were also all reruns, except for *Bordertown,* a joint venture between The Family Channel and French and Canadian investors.

Bordertown, the continuing saga of an aging U.S. marshal and a strapping young Canadian Mountie amid the late nineteenth-century border wars, was typical of Family fare to come. Neither hero drank, smoked cigarettes, nor engaged in violence or casual sex without consequences.

That December, the Family Channel announced plans to double its budget for original series and movie productions to about $100 million in 1990. Among the scheduled TV offerings were *Zorro: The Legend, Rin Tin Tin: K-9 Cop,* and *Big Brother Jake,* a sitcom starring celebrity fitness trainer Jake Steinfeld. The premiere of *Zorro* reached approximately 2 million viewers, as compared to the under 300,000 who watched the average episode of *The 700 Club* at that time.

Industry rumors spread of a restructuring, but CBN kept the details under wraps until the deal was done. On January 9, 1990, reports were issued: A newly formed corporation, International Family Entertainment (IFE), would purchase The Family Channel for $250 million. At its head, as chief executive officer, would be a reassuringly familiar face, Pat Robertson himself; Tim Robertson would be its president.

Malone, with his ample war chest and a wave of his wand, delivered Robertson from near extinction. And unlike other possible suitors, Malone—a man who habitually strong-armed irascible media titans like Ted Turner and Barry Diller into offers they couldn't refuse—had little cause to fear Robertson's controversial image.

"[Robertson] was in a position where they had to liquidate the position because it was a commercial enterprise in a non-profit church," Malone said in a 1993 Senate Judiciary Committee testimony. "And he was about to sell that company to a major broadcast network, and they were going to change the format. He actually approached us. He said, 'If you'll make an investment in my channel, I'll be able to restructure it, take it out of the church, pay the church for the channel, and retain the format.' We put up the money, we took no control at all, and we have no involvement in the management of that. And the only condition we made was that he has to keep the format a family-oriented format. That was the basis. We were carrying that channel in every one of our systems at the time that we made that arrangement."

Viewing the Family Channel as diamond in the rough, Malone had agreed to engineer 1980s Wall Street's version of divine intervention: the leveraged buyout.

In preparation, CBN hired two appraisers to assess the Family Channel's worth. The higher valuation was $250 million, the price for which Pat and Tim Robertson agreed to purchase the Family Channel. (Pat Robertson was conveniently not the chief executive of CBN when the deal went down, having handed in his resignation in 1987 in preparation for his presidential campaign.)

Rather than paying in cash, the Robertsons borrowed the entire $250 million from CBN. The resulting notes, which yield a maximum 6 percent interest rate and do not come due till 2004, were convertible into International Family Entertainment stock.

In an ingenious and perfectly legal move, Pat Robertson wagered the fortunes of the nonprofit CBN on the future growth of a brand-new public corporation.

And John Malone supplied the yeast that made the deal rise. The Robertsons needed a partner with the real capital they needed for expansion, so TCI ponied up $45 million in cash—$22 million for preferred stock in International Family Entertainment convertible into common stock (later transferred to Liberty Media Corp., a TCI subsidiary) and $23 million of the CBN convertible notes. These terms meant IFE would not have to seek bank financing, a favorable turn in an era when federal regulators were clamping down on overly speculative leverage deals.

Since its debits ($250 million of convertible notes, $22 million of preferred stock, plus the film library commitments) canceled out its assets (the estimated value of The Family Channel plus TCI's cash), IFE was arguably worth nothing at its inception.

This made it appear quaintly permissible for Pat and Tim Robertson to scoop up 4.5 million Class A common shares (with a controlling ten votes per share) of IFE stock for only 3.33 cents a share (a price ratified by an independent appraiser), or a combined total of $150,000. The Robertsons purchased another 1.5 million shares of Class B common stock (one vote per share) for $33,333, or 2.22 cents per share. Considering the fledgling IFE was worth next to nothing on paper, investing a combined total of $183,000 of their personal wealth was the least Pat Robertson, CBN's founder, and Tim Robertson, IFE's president, could do.

Dispute as one may Pat Robertson's skills in biblical prophecy (on January 1, 1980, during an all-staff prayer meeting at CBN, Pat Robertson prophesied that within two years God would violently destroy the Soviet Union and that, as Psalm 91 foretold, "we're going to see stuff crashing down around us"), his knack for foreseeing a rosy financial future was hard fact.

Two years later, in April 1992, IFE announced an initial public offering (IPO); 10 million shares of Class B common stock would be offered at $15 per share. Of those shares, 3,333,333 were sold by IFE and 6,666,667 by CBN. IFE stood to gain $50 million and CBN an impressive $100 million if all shares were sold at that price.

Clearly all IFE investors were at risk; if the company caved in, everything would be lost. But The Family Channel showed pretax profits of more than $20 million in the 12 months prior to the buyout, insurance in effect that the common stock would perform well.

Alas, the IPO was a bolter. On paper, the Robertsons had made $90 million off a $183,000 investment. And IFE's profits surged to $28 million in 1990 and $33 million in 1991. The future would be brighter. In 1995, International Family Entertainment declared revenues of $294,858,000. Its yearly net income had increased by 26 percent, from $14,792,000 in 1994 to $18,664,000 in 1995.

IFE was doing well enough in 1994 to see fit to compensate its chairman, Pat Robertson, with a salary of $440,067—"approximately 28 percent below the peer median level as revealed by the Compensation Survey data," the company's annual report fastidiously noted. (Tim Robertson, IFE's president, was paid $589,748.)

As the deal's coup de grace, Pat Robertson had ceded all his Class A shares to a tax-deferred charitable remainder trust that lists CBN as a beneficiary. On January 22, 2025, the assets of any shares that have not been sold will revert to CBN; until his death, Pat Robertson can help himself to the trust's annual income payout, which easily amounts to a few million dollars (taxable) income per year. (CBN spokespeople have boasted that the ministry and university stand to reap $600 million from the trust conversion.)

———<o>———

In the wake of its windfall, IFE went on a spending spree. During the first quarter of 1993, it bought TVS Entertainment, the British corporation that owned MTM Productions, the maker of *The Mary Tyler Moore Show, Hill Street Blues, St. Elsewhere,* and *The Bob Newhart Show.*

Founded in 1970 by Mary Tyler Moore and her then-husband Grant Tinker, MTM had been purchased by the London-based TVS five years earlier for $340 million; due to losses attributed to mismanagement, IFE snapped it up for a mere $94 million.

(An amusing footnote: The TVS deal made Pat Robertson direct partners with Harry Thomason and Linda Bloodworth-Thomason, prominent proponents of Bill Clinton. *Evening Shade,* the popular sitcom starring Burt Reynolds, is a three-way venture between MTM, CBS Entertainment, and the Thomasons. "We're always glad to welcome another member to the 'cultural elite,' " joked Harry Thomason in the *Hollywood Reporter.* "Maybe now we can get him to change his vote to Bill Clinton.")

With its reserve of over 2,000 hours of hit TV series, MTM was a choice property that dovetailed perfectly with IFE's twin desires: to make further inroads into the family-programming mainstream and to crack the European television market (via TVS).

Other deals ensued. Later that year IFE spent $20 million to acquire Calvin Gilmore Productions, a producer of country and gospel variety shows that it redubbed Great American Entertainment. In September 1993, it launched a joint venture called The Family Channel U.K., a distinctly British version of the commercial network for distribution in the United Kingdom. Soon KaloVita, a vitamin and skin cream concern, also joined the Robertson empire.

Next was the Ice Capades, the wholesome ice show franchise, which IFE took off of celebrity skater Dorothy Hamill's hands in June 1994. "We share the same fundamental goal," Hamill, who remained president, announced at a press conference in New York, "to offer high-quality entertainment that can be enjoyed by the entire family."

Loosed from the constraints of having to appear charitable, IFE, under the hand of Tim Robertson, was free to pursue all manner of profit under the rubric of family entertainment. Work began on two new channels, a fitness network called Cable Health Club (later renamed FIT-TV) and a game show block dubbed The Game Channel.

In 1994, Cable Health Club made a deal with Reebok International that *The Wall Street Journal* described as "unusual," whereby the ailing Reebok purchased a minority stake in the channel in exchange for input and product placement. The result was a new watermark in "advertorial" programming: Reebok became the sole athletic footwear and apparel sponsor on the network and began supplying equipment to all its shows.

From a business standpoint, Pat Robertson's religious and political philosophies had become irrelevant. Since 1994, when the IRS dropped an investigation into the legitimacy of the original leveraged buyout with no explanation (the IRS is not obliged to disclose the details of cases it does not take to court), International Family Entertainment has flourished, unencumbered by the specter of impropriety.

The recent hiring of Anthony Thomopoulos, formerly of Steven Spielberg's Amblin Television, to head MTM Entertainment bespoke further legitimization of the "family" network. In early 1996 alone, four big-name Hollywood TV stars signed on with The Family Channel to star in or produce films for The Family Channel—Robert Urich (*Vega$*), John Schneider (*The Dukes of Hazzard*), Donna Mills (*Knots Landing*), and Jaclyn Smith (*Charlie's Angels*).

"I put out the word to my agents some time ago to look for parts in films I could watch with my kids without being uncomfortable," Urich told one reporter. "I don't want to see another script about husbands murdering wives or fathers having sex with their children."

———<o>———

Pat Robertson's turnaround had been nothing short of remarkable.

As a corporate entity Robertson was well beyond opprobrium. And today International Family Entertainment, thanks principally to the continued prosperity of The Family Channel, stands on its own merits.

Robertson, like all true American capitalists, had developed a quality product, a unique, superior commodity that he could mass market and make affordable to the average consumer.

The United States was already the most religious of the industrial nations, so why not reward the people with a shiny new product to validate their devotions?

"This is a business like no other in that Robertson markets a little piece of heaven," offered Jonathan Hudson, an independent researcher.

In essence, Pat Robertson had done for the American psyche what Ray Kroc of McDonald's once did for the American palate. Robertson's Big Mac was his own brand of nondenominational Christianity. And the "special sauce" was an especially zesty dab: a hint at the promise of the wonderful life beyond. And no matter where you were or who you were, it would be as reliable as Kroc's "two all-beef patties": It would look, feel, and taste the same way, every time.

———<o>———

It was a miracle on the order of the ones he often told his viewers about. Pat Robertson had in a moment crossed the line from one world to another. In the old world, he was an also-ran religious and political figure plagued by allegations of financial impropriety and a dwindling capital base. But on one fateful day in April 1992, the day of IFE's prodigiously profitable IPO, Robertson wholly and heartily stepped into a magnificent new world.

In the new world, Pat Robertson was a businessman first and foremost, and a damn smart one at that. That didn't mean he would deny his faith or his conservative mien, simply that he was blameless, forgiven. The fully transformed Pat Robertson was clean and prosperous. Reborn, one might say.

"We've never regarded ourselves competitors with anybody in the religious field," Pat Robertson could confidently declare in 1995. "While we're working on programs, it's the secular people that we're out basically trying to excel or beat."

This was true. In order to compete in the broader marketplace, Robertson—as chairman of IFE, now more beholden to his stockholders than to his flock—needed to put profit number one, well ahead of relatively unprofitable ventures such as spreading the word and engaging in charitable operations.

If his activities since 1992 are any gauge, Pat Robertson has adjusted splendidly to the responsibilities of his new job. Scanning the globe for diversified expansion prospects, he has targeted mostly undervalued media properties with an excellent chance for growth.

In 1995 alone, Robertson considered and rejected the possibilities of buying Pakistan Mobile Communication from Motorola and, in a deal apart from CBN or IFE, *The Houston Post* from its current owners. (A few years back he contemplated bailing out another reputable news gatherer, the ailing United Press International, for $6 million—he instead decided to start his own Standard News.)

Among his 1995 international winnings were a 40 percent stake in Asia Pacific Media Corporation (Robertson's charitable trust bought another 20 percent), a company devoted to investing in cable and satellite operators in the Pacific Rim area and an ample chunk of China Entertainment Television Broadcast, a 24-hour "no sex, no violence, and no news" satellite channel broadcast in Mandarin and beamed to 28 million subscribers in China by Hong Kong businessman Robert Chua.

In July CBN hired the Haskell Company of Jacksonville, Florida, to construct a $65 million, 250-unit retirement community on Virginia Beach called Founders Village, pointing the way to another possible market for the future.

The surest sign of how well IFE is doing may be its ordinariness quotient as an investment option. Managers at some of the nation's most popular and reputable mutual fund groups have embraced IFE stock, traded on the New York Stock Exchange, as a solid growth security. If you own shares in funds run by Schwab, T. Rowe Price, Vanguard, or Royce, you may already be benefiting from Pat Robertson's business acuity. Mario Gabelli, the swashbuckling head of the highly esteemed Gabelli Funds, liked IFE's prospects so much he gobbled up around 13 percent of its stock and named the company as one of the ten most likely candidates for a corporate takeover in 1996.

In the October 1995 issue of *Worth* magazine, Ralph Wanger and Chuck McQuaid, managers of The Acorn Fund, described IFE as one of their favorite domestic stocks. They cited its 20 percent growth in cash flow and 60 percent growth in net income as salient factors, "despite startup costs associated with the new Cable Health Club network and the U.K. Family Channel." But in every other respect this was a rave: "Right now," said Wanger and McQuaid, "investors who buy stock in this company essentially get these startup channels for free—not to mention a valuable film library, a production company, and live-entertainment assets. If the new channels develop as I [*sic*] expect, the stock could double in a few years." The item made no mention of Pat Robertson.

Although the formal separation of the for-profit IFE and the non-profit CBN guaranteed an arm's-length relationship in perpetuity, having Pat Robertson as their common link has made for some convenient swapping of capital. For example, IFE secured $150 million in credit through the Bank of Boston in 1993 to repurchase over $55 million convertible notes, which had been converted into shares of IFE Class B common stock before purchase, from Regent University.

———◦———

For the faithful, to see the heads of the various Robertson-helmed organizations standing around the boss on his sixty-fifth birthday must have further confirmed that his cup overfloweth. After all, Pat Robertson knew how to run things.

If Robertson could spark a profitable corporation, one could only imagine what bounty his perspicacity had shed upon his missionary effort. Operation Blessing was founded by Robertson in 1978 to create "healthy communities which allow people to be reconciled to God by helping meet basic human needs of the urban poor and disaster victims globally, and by assisting individuals, families and neighborhoods to become self-sufficient."

The symbol of that munificence in 1995 would be the "flying hospital," an L-1011 jumbo jet decked out with $16 million worth of surgical suites and classrooms designed to deliver modern medicine to Third World countries. Robertson had regaled *700 Club* viewers for many months with reduced-scale models of the plane, explaining how costly such a wonderful project could be.

Not that Operation Blessing hadn't been resourceful. The organization had purchased the L-1011 for a mere $4 million, a bargain sum for the 1974 Lockheed (Delta replaced its fleet of L-1011s with newer jets costing around $100 million each).

By keeping its overhead costs low in 1995, Operation Blessing, according to its own reports, had used an income of $36 million to distribute over 17 million pounds of food, via its Hunger Strike Force trucks, to Americans in need. Indeed the organization took credit with providing "more than 24 million people" worldwide with sustenance and supplies.

But 1996 found Operation Blessing in deep financial straits. The charitable organization started the year by laying off 22 of its 67 employees and pulling 12 of its 14 tractor-trailer rigs out of service.

A new Operation Blessing president, Paul C. Thompson, explained to reporters in January that his nonprofit group, like many charitable organizations, had suffered from declining contributions in recent years.

Although Robertson had spun off Operation Blessing as a nonprofit group independent from CBN in 1993, Thompson revealed that CBN had supplied Operation Blessing with $20 million of its $36 million 1995 budget. It turns out the organization grew too rapidly, expanding from 13 to 70 employees in two years.

"My job really is to kind of kick-start Operation Blessing, redefine its mission, help it become a fully independent entity," Thompson said. "We are going to move away from dependence upon CBN and move toward an expanded resource base."

Meanwhile, plans for the "flying hospital" surged ahead. "There are people who are caught up with the vision of this plane and what it can do, and they are people of means," said Thompson.

Thompson, hired the previous June to render Operation Blessing more self-sufficient, worried only that keeping the jet in the air might absorb the bulk of Operation Blessing's budget.

It was a lesson hard learned: Charity donors rarely loosen their purse strings with quite the same flourish as the stockholders of a burgeoning corporate giant.

CHAPTER FOUR

On the Campus

On I-64, the interstate that hustles visitors past strip malls, fast-food joints, and gas stations, far inland from the Virginia Beach oceanfront, the only sign pointing the way to Robertson Central reads simply "Regent University." But it's the gargantuan Founders Inn, Robertson's 249-room luxury hotel and conference center, that sits at the front of the property, facing the road.

Pat Robertson's 11-building complex in Virginia Beach, Virginia, only further blurs the boundaries between his secular and nonsecular entities. Robertson purchased the 685 acres in 1976; on October 6, 1979, CBN's studio headquarters opened its doors.

Although Founders Inn, owned by IFE and operated by an outside hotel chain, is the site's newest building its Federal-style redbrick-and-white-steeple architecture matches that of the others exactly. Except that it's much bigger.

Built on 26 acres, Founders is prepared to accommodate business groups of up to 1,400 with meeting rooms, tennis courts, and two pools, indoors and outdoors.

Prominently displayed in the Founders Inn lobby are oil reproduction portraits of George Washington, John Adams, and James Madison; tucked in a corner is a more recent original of Robertson, pictured against an American flag backdrop.

Regardless of past trouble over hiring practices that discriminated against non-Christians, there are relatively few oblique references to religion at Founders. (In deference to rising profits, the hotel bar even began serving alcohol recently, reversing what was once one of the temperate Robertson's biggest no-nos.)

Quite the contrary at CBN studio headquarters. Although its grand front steps, Washington-scale facade, and majestic white columns suggest a county courthouse, the building itself is shaped like a cross. Inscribed above the front portal are the words "This Gospel of the Kingdom shall be preached in all the world for a witness unto all nations" from Matthew 24:14.

Designed by architect Archie Royal Davis, a colonial-period expert, the edifice incorporates Indiana limestone and James River–style bricks to a heady but bizarrely anachronistic effect.

In harsh violation of its neoclassical airs, the facility houses two hulking, state-of-the-art soundstages, one in each arm of the cross-beam. The effect is that of an airplane hangar as it might have been designed for the grounds of Colonial Williamsburg.

I arrived late one afternoon at CBN to meet with one of Regent University's founding faculty members, a professor in the School of Communication and Arts, who had agreed to show me around.

Our communiqué had begun via e-mail a few months earlier, whereby he wrote me at first that Robertson's office had advised him not to grant the interview. But after only a little bit of cyber-prodding, he agreed to be interviewed by phone under the sole condition that his name not be mentioned in print.

My professor turned out to be friendly and open, afterwards insisting that I sit in on one of his classes, an evening videotaping for a half-hour drama episode his students were producing for a Dutch client, when I visited.

"Nobody knows you at CBN, do they?" he had asked the final time we spoke before my arrival, the only other sign of nervousness he displayed about my visit.

In person, he was outgoing and quiescent. A tall, broad-faced man with a splotchy brush of facial hair who sculpts his curly salt-and-pepper hair into a pompadour. In no way did he exude the pinched pleasantries that frequently supplanted genuine friendliness during my stay. Truly nothing about his appearance—not his faded jeans or tatty tweed jacket, his collarless shirt or black Reeboks—fit my expectations.

He is a Roman Catholic, he explained, a distinct minority (approximately 10 percent) at both CBN and Regent. That differentness seemed to translate into an almost puckish school boy's verve, the professor's not-so-subtle way of communicating that, in his case—for reasons of semantics and seniority—each and every house rule didn't necessarily apply.

We entered Studio 6 through a side entrance, where a lone security guard glanced at my host's security pass from behind glass as he waved me through.

As the cast members and crew trickled from the dressing room into the studio, I was struck by how—well—how secular everything seemed. The teacher joked around with the cameramen, his pupils, with whom he'd gone out drinking the night before after an 11:00 P.M. wrap. Someone's shrimp pie had given a few of the men the runs the night before—cause, predictably, for a hearty round of bodily-function jokes, sans the usual obscenities.

While the students readied brand-new Sony cameras on a living-room set (left over from *Another Life*, CBN's mid-eighties Christian soap opera) at the center of a composite floor easily spanning the yardage of a football field, we toured the other sets on the floor's perimeter.

In one corner was the set for CBN's Middle East programming; in another, the one for an in-the-works Sunday edition of *The 700 Club*. Both were decorated in dark woods and oriental rugs. The oriental-rug motif seems to be a popular one at Robertson's compound; the white marble floor in the lobby is swathed in magnificently expansive Persian.

My guess is the rugs are a short-hand way of communicating "wealth lives here," or some such corollary. There's really no need for the underscoring.

Tonight the students commanded three brand-new Sony video cameras that glided soundlessly across the perfectly level studio floor. Around the bend, in the studio's control room, others sat at fully computerized consoles in front of a bank of television monitors. Some control boards sat idle, giving those students who aren't working a place to put their feet up during sessions that have been running from 5 to 11 each night.

Regent secured a $65,000 grant to produce 13 half-hour teleplays from Lumen 2000, an evangelical Catholic media concern funded by Dutch millionaire and charismatic Piet Dirksen that once engineered a worldwide television broadcast of a recitation by Pope John Paul II.

The professor described the shows as "modern parables," none of which is overtly religious. "There's a sci-fi one," he said, "there's one done in the roaring twenties."

Lumen 2000 originally intended to start its own production company in Holland, but found Regent with its stable of cheap talent, students eager to be scriptwriters, directors, and producers, to be more suitable to its budget.

Regent students generated 75 scripts of which 13 were chosen for production. The university hired professional actors at its own expense.

Although my host explained it more than once, I'd have one hell of a time trying to explain the financial relationship between the television programs and the class they're supposedly the course work for. The half-hour episodes are being paid for by the client, the professor told me, but the university is renting space from CBN.

"But isn't CBN nonprofit also?" I wondered out loud.

"CBN is just the name for the umbrella organization," he assured.

To confuse matters even more, it's mostly students manning the equipment, but the actors are all professionals, hired in casting calls. For the purposes of the production, the professor is known as executive producer.

As I mulled over the discrepancies, I was treated to an informal tour of the grounds.

Studio 7, where *The 700 Club* broadcasts live from five days a week, is Studio 6's mirror image, except it houses even more state-of-the-art equipment.

"Go on, sit in his seat," my host said, with an impish glee. Once I was comfortably resting in Robertson's chair on *The 700 Club*'s living room set, I was treated to a short, secular confessional. "Pat can be really mean," the professor whispered to me. "He has a habit of using people and then getting rid of them."

A Regent journalism professor later provided me with an example. A member of *The 700 Club*'s technical support staff, he said, once fouled up a simple task. Robertson blew his top and ordered his dismissal, said he never wanted to see this guy again. Others present felt the punishment didn't fit the crime, so the employee was transferred to a different part of the operation where Robertson would "never see him again." The wrongdoer still works at CBN today.

The CBN counseling center—the first of its kind and, according to lore, the heart of the Robertson's ministry—is on the building's second floor, above the studios. A horseshoe-shaped ring of cubicles is visible from behind glass, virtually all of which are empty. Although the center is a 24-hour facility, monitored primarily by volunteers offering prayer and advice to anyone who calls in, only a few carrels are filled this evening. "It's hard to get volunteers to come in late at night," the professor explained. Inevitably, paid employees sit out the wee hours.

On the same floor, behind closed doors, is CBN's telemarketing engine, where representatives dial out to solicit funds, rather than waiting for the phones to ring.

————◀◦▶————

Outside the building, we march past a gas-lighted flame in the turn-around. "That's a pretty recent addition," the professor told me.

"What's its significance?" I asked.

"Oh, I think it's just Pat's JFK obsession," he responded. Then, after a pause, "It's a good effect, though, don't you think?"

If business, not religion, is ostensibly the primary focus of what transpires at studio headquarters, the next morning's tour easily eroded this notion. After leading a quick prayer session in the studio chapel, a perky guide named Glenda hurried us past the studios and counseling center, which was now brimming with busy counselors, mostly young African-American women, in order to explicate the religious artwork that lines the hallways opposite the broadcasting hub.

Modern paintings rendered in meticulously neo-Renaissance style, such as a 28-foot-wide Last Supper, each constituted yet another opportunity to proselytize.

As we idled in front of a smaller, conspicuously primitive painting of Jesus, Glenda asked us to gaze into the figure's eyes. "See the way they kind of glow?" she said in a soft Southern drawl. "This painting gives us a real idea of just how much Jesus loves us."

CHAPTER FIVE

---◄◊►---

The Beginning

Absalom Willis Robertson, Pat Robertson's father, served in the U.S. Senate for three consecutive terms, from 1948 to 1966. During those years, the Senator resided primarily in the janitor's room of a downtown Washington hotel, alone.

I recently made the three-and-half-hour drive from Washington to Lexington, Virginia, Pat Robertson's hometown, in part to get an idea of the distance his father needed to travel in order to visit his family. I also went to obtain a sense of the other Pat Robertson, the Pat Robertson from before fundamentalist Christianity changed his life's course.

Indeed, at every turn, Lexington offers curious hints at the man Pat Robertson might have been.

While in Washington, I dropped in on Charles R. McDowell, a friend of Robertson's from childhood, in his cozy corner office at the National Press Building. McDowell is a Washington-based political correspondent of some renown for the *Richmond Times-Dispatch*.

One of the first things Charlie McDowell told me was that he was perfectly willing to talk about Pat Robertson and himself as friends in the past, but that he wished to avoid any situations that would create "a conflict of interest with my covering politics, my being a columnist who's free to take positions, my position being pretty much anti-Christian Coalition."

In his denim shirt, wide-wale corduroys and sweater vest, McDowell was, in outward presentation, the direct antithesis of Pat Robertson.

A first-rate raconteur, his easy demeanor and hearty laugh only slightly concealed an unabashed intellect.

As he spoke, he fumbled with his thick glasses like an absent-minded college professor. (In fact, McDowell's father was a law professor at Washington and Lee.) And yet as McDowell recounted the years he shared with Robertson growing up (in a deep, crisp "mountain" southern accent that has gotten him voice-over work in Ken Burns documentaries), the commonalities began cropping up.

Although McDowell is a few years older than Robertson, his first recollections of his old friend were as a very precocious toddler. "I have known him all the way from some sort of preschool class in some lady's living room out near his house when all the rest of us were about five," he said. "Lexington had a freak thing that you couldn't go to school till you were seven—no one's quite sure why. So I must have been six or seven, and here was this three-year-old, Pat, and he was just as smart as the rest of us."

Except for a period when McDowell was in the Navy and Robertson attended the McCallie prep school in Chattanooga (not incidentally, Ted Turner's alma mater, too) for his last two years of high school, the two remained close. As undergraduates at Washington and Lee University in Lexington, McDowell proposed Robertson as a member of the Sigma Alpha Epsilon fraternity, "and he was a popular member," he recalled. When McDowell got married in his wife-to-be's home, Pat Robertson offered to play photographer at the wedding.

"He was congenial, he was kind of plump—he could do sports okay, but it wasn't his face," McDowell continued. "He was good in school—bright, extremely bright. As far as I could tell, he wanted to be a lawyer. . . . Pat was ambitious, so he wanted to be a *big* lawyer, a *big* investor, a *big* something."

Because the Robertsons lived at 502 Highland Road in a big yellow clapboard house overlooking what was then the town's high school (now Wadell Elementary School), many assumed that the famous senator and his family were rather well off. The Robertsons had built the house in 1929 on two acres in an apple orchard. But as a United States senator, Willis Robertson made a modest $10,000 a year, though still enough to employ a cook and a maid in post-Depression-era Virginia.

Gladys Robertson, Pat's mother, did not want to live in Washington and A. Willis Robertson could hardly afford to trek back and forth from the capital. So the senator spent his weeks in Washington lodging in a room below the lobby level in the Dodge Hotel. And Mrs. Robertson stayed in the house in Lexington with Pat and his older brother, Taddy.

"We weren't dealing with fancy people," McDowell observed. "We were dealing with bright, nice people."

However, the young Pat Robertson always had a streak of the promoter in him. Said McDowell: "I always got the impression that Pat didn't like having to sort of skimp along while his father was off to Washington."

What the Robertsons lacked in funds, however, they more than made up for in breeding. A. Willis Robertson could claim, through his mother, Josephine Ragland Willis, a lineage that stretched back to the Gordons of Scotland. James Gordon, who immigrated from Scotland to Lancaster County in 1738, participated in the drafting of the Constitution.

Benjamin Harrison, a member of the Continental Congress, a signer of the Declaration of Independence, and later the governor of Virginia, was a relative of both the Gordon and Willis families. The Robertsons also traced their lineage to two presidents, William Henry Harrison and Benjamin Harrison, and the Churchill family.

Born in Martinsburg, West Virginia, in 1887, the son of an educated Baptist minister and grandson of a Civil War hero, A. Willis Robertson grew up as one of six children in western Virginia. He graduated from the first high school in Franklin County, established in part by his mother. He entered Richmond College at age 16 and subsequently obtained bachelor's degrees in both history and law in five years.

As an undergraduate at Richmond, Willis Robertson developed an intense admiration for native Virginian Woodrow Wilson, whom he regarded as an early and leading proponent for lasting international peace.

Robertson passed the bar in 1908 and took up private practice as a member of the private Buena Vista, Virginia, law firm Willis and Robertson. In 1910, he moved to Lexington. But when Woodrow

Wilson, then governor of New Jersey, declared his candidacy for the Democratic presidential nomination in 1912, Robertson decided to become a delegate to the Virginia Democratic convention.

The positive experience apparently awakened an ancestral pull toward public service. In 1915, Robertson was elected to the Virginia State Senate. Henry Flood Byrd, later the governor of Virginia and a United States senator alongside Robertson, took a seat next to his Virginia colleague the same year. For Robertson, a brief volunteer stint as an infantryman in World War I was to be the only pause in an otherwise uninterrupted and successful political career.

As a representative of Virginia's seventh district, Robertson distinguished himself primarily as a conservationist, playing a substantial role in the formation of a Select Committee on Conservation of Wild Life Resources. A lifelong hunter (he was voted Outstanding Sportsman of America by *Field & Stream* magazine in 1926), Robertson gained an early reputation as an independent-thinking conservative Democrat. Taxation problems were a particular obsession.

Although Willis Robertson and Harry Byrd had been born weeks apart in Martinsburg and remained close colleagues (in 1926, as governor, Byrd made Robertson chairman of the State Commission of Game and Inland Fisheries and a member of the gubernatorial cabinet), Robertson did not share his compatriot's views closely enough to want to trail along as Byrd's power grew.

When Senator Carter Glass died in 1946, Virginia Democrats chose the widely respected Representative Robertson to complete his term. A. Willis Robertson subsequently served three consecutive terms as a U.S. senator.

Senator Robertson concurred with his conservative congressional colleagues on many issues. He voted consistently against federal expansion and increased federal spending, except when Virginia stood to benefit. He engineered legislation to oppose organized labor and stood against the Supreme Court's 1954 decision on public school desegregation (on constitutional rather than on racial grounds).

A Mason, a charter member of the Lexington post of the American Legion, and the chairman of the Senate's mighty Banking and Currency Committee, Willis Robertson was the virtual embodiment of establishment virtue. Viewed by opponents as an unbending tightwad, the senator nevertheless enjoyed a regular-guy reputation among his peers and fellow Lexingtonians.

In Congress, however, his steadfast refusal to act as a cog in the Byrd machine distinguished him. Although an early supporter of Franklin D. Roosevelt's New Deal, Robertson ultimately opposed the New Deal's far-reaching social programs, and he thus eventually alienated Harry Byrd, a tight Roosevelt ally. Some reports portray Byrd as having tried to bounce Robertson out in 1954, but the well-liked senator (he won his third term in 1960 with 81 percent of the vote) remained in office until 1966, when he was defeated in the Democratic primary by a new-era congressman, William Spong.

A. Willis Robertson married Gladys Churchill Willis, his first cousin, in 1920. Born in Florida and raised in Alabama, Gladys Robertson apparently cast a more enigmatic shadow than her gregarious, transparent husband. Ten years younger than the senator, Gladys Robertson was, by all accounts, well-dressed and well-mannered—the perfect hostess and a born conversationalist (she was especially known for her long phone calls).

Although loath to live in Washington, Mrs. Robertson read most of the senator's speeches before he delivered them. Inspirational messages which she culled from the Bible were frequently used in the Senate prayer group and sometimes even wound up in the Congressional Record.

"I met her many times," said McDowell. "And what you had was an aristocratic grace." She and her husband attended Lexington's Manly Memorial Baptist Church, a large domed cathedral-like building on Lexington's Main Street, in a small town where many others attended either the Presbyterian or Episcopalian church.

A Hollins College graduate, the daughter of a trial lawyer who retired and became a Baptist minister, Mrs. Robertson was known as a roundly elegant yet kind soul. And yet as the years passed, and the distance between her and her husband grew, she became intensely religious and withdrawn.

More than one Lexington acquaintance recalled the first time Pat returned home to visit his mother with his new wife, Adelia, and infant son, Timothy. Timothy had been conceived out of wedlock, a fact unearthed by the press during Pat Robertson's 1988 run for the

Republican nomination but common knowledge for years among close acquaintances. Gladys Robertson refused her son and his new family at her threshold, insisting instead that they stay at a hotel in town.

"It wasn't a sternness, particularly, it was just a sense of betrayal or hurt—it just took her a while to accept that," said Matthew Paxton, another Lexington friend. "It takes a little disengaging there anyway, under the best of circumstances."

Because A. Willis Robertson was already 43 years old and away in Washington when his second son, Marion Gordon "Pat" Robertson, was born on March 22, 1930, Pat's closest bond developed with his mother. The Robertsons' other son, known as Taddy (né A. Willis Jr.), was more than six years Pat's senior and already out in the world by the time Pat was a teenager.

"Pat never quite had enough money and he was always looking for summer jobs and something to do," Charlie McDowell recalled. "Pat wanted to hustle."

One summer, one of Pat's entrepreneurial schemes was successful enough that the Lexington town sheriff took it upon himself to squelch it. The young senator's son had been selling football betting cards to students and townies, with odds reportedly purloined from a local bookie with ties to the Mafia. The youngest Robertson curtailed the endeavor as soon as the sheriff kindly but firmly explained to him this kind of activity could be extremely detrimental to his father's political reputation.

Charlie McDowell was considerably surprised when he first heard that Pat Robertson had joined the ministry. After all, McDowell knew Pat Robertson essentially as a gregarious fraternity brother and as the friend of his game enough to play photographer at McDowell's wedding.

"Pat was a member of a church-going family and I think he went to Sunday school," McDowell said, "but I think if you had given any of us twenty possible jobs that he would have had in life that the preacher would have been down around number sixteen, seventeen, or eighteen. Pat sounded like an adventurer as a kid, and an intellectual."

Various accounts of Robertson's college years portray the young Lexingtonian as anything but religious. His brother Tad told the *Roanoke Times & World-News* in 1987 that Pat had contemplated resigning from SAE his senior year because many of his brethren, older World War II veterans returning to school, were too serious for his tastes. "He was bored with his nonpartying fraternity brothers," the older sibling explained. Robbin L. Gates, a retired history professor, recalled Robertson inviting Gates's wife-to-be to christen his new car with a half-pint bottle of bourbon.

"What I wasn't surprised at was that it was a kind of ministry that took advantage of his public personality," McDowell said, "his ease in public, his love of show business, his congeniality, all those things—what I considered the more positive sides of Pat."

In 1949, McDowell headed for New York to attend Columbia University's graduate school of journalism. One time while McDowell was in New York, Pat Robertson visited him and the two took in the ballet and a Broadway show. Knowing full well what the proper southern boy's response ought to be, Robertson joked that he much preferred Broadway—the production was *Gentlemen Prefer Blondes* starring Carol Channing—to the "tippy-toe dancers."

————◇————

In Lexington, I talked to the retired editor and former owner of the town's newspaper (and another Columbia Journalism grad), Matthew W. Paxton III. An old college buddy and fraternity brother of Robertson's, Paxton has a family history typical of Lexington. Paxton's father was a leading lawyer in town who had inherited the weekly paper, today called the *News-Gazette,* from his father.

When Matt Paxton greeted me at the top of the long, winding driveway that leads to his home, a majestic 200-year-old farmhouse on the far edge of town, he was wearing a floppy wide-brimmed leather cowpoke's hat.

Inside the house, dressed in a biscuit-colored cardigan, Paxton cut a more aristocratic figure. A soft-spoken and eloquent man with distinguished snowy white hair and a carefully trimmed mustache who also happens to be a graduate of Columbia Journalism, he nonetheless apologized for his southern accent, fretting that it would get garbled on my tape recorder. "It always sounds like grits and cornpone—it sounds *stupid,* I think," he said with a gentle chuckle.

The Paxtons in fact counted themselves among the town's more prominent clans, along with the McDowells, the Robertsons, and the Glasgows. Matt Paxton's father duck-hunted with Senator Robertson, and young Matt saw a lot of the senator's son in informal settings, such as the neighborhood mock orange wars that ensued whenever enough mock oranges had fallen from the trees near the high school.

Because he, too, was a few years older, Matt Paxton didn't become close friends with Pat Robertson till college.

"He was always a little precocious and big for his age, though," Paxton said, "so he tended to run with people who were a little bit older."

It was as W&L classmates and SAE fraternity brothers that Paxton and Robertson became close. One summer the senator helped both boys get summer jobs with the National Park Service out west. Matt was stationed in the white pine forests of northern Idaho while Pat secured a position at Yellowstone Park.

"He was actually supposed to be pumping gas," Paxton told me, "but he very quickly became an entrepreneur and rented out his little cabin to tourists and ended up doing much better than he otherwise would have."

————◄o►————

To the outsider's eye, Lexington appears to be an old southern hick town, albeit a moderately well-to-do one. Neatly tended nineteenth-century redbrick buildings crowd narrow Main Street.

Founded in 1778, Lexington is home to 6,959 people, two institutions of higher learning, nine churches, and one movie theater. The town is best characterized by its twin patron saints, Civil War generals Thomas J. "Stonewall" Jackson and Robert E. Lee—both of whom are entombed within the town's borders—and its unduly stringent two-hour parking regulations.

But it is easy to scratch below that surface. The campuses of Washington and Lee University, Robertson's alma mater, and the Virginia Military Institute are wedged smack against each other in the center of the two hilly square miles that comprise Lexington. Both have fueled a steady influx of professors and students from around the country and the world for over a hundred years.

Stonewall Jackson taught natural philosophy at VMI from 1851, for a decade; in 1861 and 1862 he led the Confederate troops in both battles of Bull Run; in 1863, he was accidentally killed by his own troops in the Battle of Chancellorsville.

During the Civil War, Union troops razed the buildings at VMI but spared those at the neighboring Washington College, out of respect for George Washington, who had made a substantial gift to the school in 1796.

In 1865, Robert E. Lee was made president of Washington College and built himself a house on the grounds of the handsome Georgian-style redbrick campus. After Lee died, the school was renamed Washington and Lee.

A good number of Washington and Lee alumni from Pat Robertson's era (Robertson graduated magna cum laude with a history degree in 1950) went on to lead powerful, public lives. Virginia senator John Warner, former Virginia governor Linwood Holton, Ronald Reagan's secretary of labor William Brock, newscaster Roger Mudd, novelist Tom Wolfe, football hero Walt Michaels, Hollywood director Fielder Cook, and former Washington and Lee president Robert Huntley all matriculated the school during that time.

"It was a real hotbed of people that did pretty well," as Charlie McDowell put it, "and were all just in that little college together."

Pat Robertson, like Charlie McDowell, Matt Paxton, and most W&L students from Lexington, lived at home while attending college. He palled around with campus leaders but displayed little interest in real politics.

Today Washington and Lee and VMI still retain their distinct characters. Washington and Lee is a traditional private liberal arts college with attractive Georgian-style redbrick buildings and a pretty, tree-lined campus. It went fully coed in 1984 and recently built a state-of-the-art performance center.

The buildings at Virginia Military Institute, in contrast, are stark, drab green monstrosities. Still resolutely all-male, the state-supported VMI was recently embroiled in a sex discrimination suit filed by a young female recruit.

Before World War II, the rivalry between the two schools was so fierce that intramural baseball was canceled due to fighting between the teams.

Matt Paxton drove me around Lexington in his rickety, gray Oldsmobile, pointing out the town's sites. At the center of the Stonewall Jackson Memorial Cemetery stands a statue of its revered namesake. (Senator Robertson was buried here when he died in 1971, after a funeral service at VMI.) After his death, Robert E. Lee's home remained the residence for the Washington and Lee's president; Lee was buried in a crypt within the campus chapel.

"To some extent, Pat always kept his own council, played his cards a little close," Paxton opined. "He gives the impression of being a great extrovert, very gracious and very friendly with a ready smile, but when it's all said and done, I think he's always been a private person."

As my tour of Lexington comes to a close, I wonder out loud how many local residents abide by Pat Robertson's heady brew of old-time religion and aggressive social engineering. "I don't think there are too many people who are exactly of his persuasion, that conservative. Most of the folks here are pretty mainline in their religious affiliations, I think."

"It wasn't Andy Griffith's Mayberry," said Julia Martin, another friend of Robertson's from high school, of Lexington. "It was a lot more cosmopolitan than that."

Pat Robertson's only year at Lexington High School was as a sophomore (he spent ninth grade at the McDonough School, a military prep in Baltimore, and graduated from McCallie); during that year, he starred in a production of Gilbert and Sullivan's *H.M.S. Pinafore* in which Martin, then a sophomore, played Buttercup.

"Pat was perfect as the Captain in the *Pinafore*," recalled Martin, today a stocky, energetic spark plug of a senior citizen. "He looked the part because he was tall and he was big, and he wore that great, big plumed hat."

Although Martin grew up attending Manly Baptist Church with the Robertsons, she, too, was surprised by Pat's religious conversion. "I was aware of his mother's deep commitment to her faith, to her Bible," said Martin, who recalled Gladys Robertson as bearing a striking resemblance to the Good Witch in *The Wizard of Oz* (as played by

Billie Burke in the 1938 classic). "She had that sweet little voice and her hair was kind of fluffy and golden."

Mrs. Robertson believed her son could do anything he set his mind to, a sentiment Martin was inclined to agree with. "Pat has always had beautiful manners," Martin said. "He's never been pushy, he's always been smooth-talking, not glib. He's disarming."

In the course of her talk with me, Julia Martin bared her conservative credentials. The former high school cheerleader went on to work in the press office of VMI for 40 years. She made it clear that she disapproved of the recent effort to terminate VMI's status as a state-supported all-male institution. Yet even Martin mustered a hearty laugh when I asked her about Robertson's 1988 bid for the presidency.

"I don't watch *The 700 Club*," she explained, "even though it's someone I know. I have mixed emotions about evangelists who venture into the political world."

Chapter Six

Thursday Morning,
March 21, 1996,
Studio 7,
Virginia Beach, Virginia

One Thursday morning in March, I showed up 9:30 sharp at CBN headquarters, hoping to catch a live broadcast of *The 700 Club*. Upon my arrival, I was quickly and unexpectedly corralled into the chapel, a circular, domed white room with a larger-than-life wooden cross suspended from its center. There a young, apple-cheeked pastor with a dark mustache and toothy smile was preaching to the other audience standbys, today a ruddy-looking senior couple from Idaho and two scrawny middle-aged women in high-necked print dresses. The subject of today's preshow sermon was the nature of God's love. The concept was such a difficult one to grasp, he estimated, because loving God required total submission, behavior not often associated with health and strength. Yet that, in effect, was what the Lord required. As example, the minister told a story of how one night he and his four-year-old daughter, whom he and his wife had been painstakingly training in moral virtue, sat down to watch *Star Trek: The Next Generation* together, "and almost immediately, she said, 'Daddy, that's bad.'" He told us how at first he was angry because he so enjoyed watching the program, but upon reflection he changed his mind. "I had noticed the way some New Age stuff had begun creeping into the show's plots," he explained. Needless to say, he soon came to understand his daughter's unerring purity had pinpointed the show's satanic undertones. He hadn't watched the show since. By show time, ten of us had accumulated. On the other side of the studio's metal detector, an aide arranged us and rearranged us, searching for a pattern that would make the few seem like many through the camera lens. Singles (like me) were paired together to look like couples. The warm-up talent, a jolly, corpulent man who collected questions for the "stump Pat" segment of the show, reminded us to smile a lot and applaud on cue. Within minutes, Pat Robertson and Terry Meeuwsen, barely acknowledging the audience, had silently strolled onto the floor and taken their places on the "Newswatch Today" set. Thicker and more tired-looking in person—with his slight hunch and distinctive features caricatured by age he looks very much like the routed Richard Nixon in his final years—Robertson nonetheless lighted up, the hard wrinkles of his face magically smoothing out into his familiar chipmunk grin, as soon as the cameras began whirring. But the split-second the first story, an update on gun control legislation, went to a taped video segment, Robertson shifted moods. "That promotion was terrible!" he barked at no one in particular. "Who wrote that?" he yelled, as his face curled into a scowl. "The promotion should be better than the story, not worse!" For the next five minutes Robertson browbeat the floor director, who began anxiously pacing back and forth as Robertson continued his rant through the full five-minute break. Meeuwsen maintained her radiant composure through the whole episode. Seemingly oblivious to the audience, Robertson spent the other intermissions eating candies out of a dish, legs crossed, chair back, cordovan loafers high in the air. Even during the question-and-answer segment of the program, where Robertson gives off-the-top-of-his-head Bible-based advice to audience members and callers-in, he faces away from the bleachers, at the camera in the studio corner instead of the questioners. Only while watching a pretaped born-again testimony segment featuring NFL wide receiver Irving Fryer does Robertson flash any hint of having a good time, chortling and clapping his hands every time Fryer punctuates a paean to the Lord with the word "man" (as in, "God is everything to me, man"). After the broadcast, Robertson and Meeuwsen walked to our end of the studio and thanked everyone for coming. "Happy birthday, Pat!" burst out one audience member, a long-haired young man in jeans with enough pious zeal to have kept his leather-bound Bible open for the course of the show. "Thanks," said Robertson, with a presidential wave of his arm. "They're going to be roasting me this Saturday in

Los Angeles. Larry King's the emcee." As Robertson made his brisk exit, the well-wisher added, "Make sure to save him, Pat!"

———◇———

The Family Channel doesn't sell advertising for the three and a half hours each day devoted to *The 700 Club*. This is because the "Pat Robertson Show," as it easily could be called, is the principal lasting legacy of the nonprofit CBN. Although *The 700 Club* is pitched during its annual January telethon and in the countless fundraising mailings it issues throughout the year as the conservative antidote to government-supported public broadcasting, it is in effect a religious infomercial. In the early 1970s, when CBN first solicited commercials, Pat Robertson learned the hard way that secular advertising and religious programming did not comfortably mix. Back then, national ad reps had a word for Christian programs like *The 700 Club:* They called them "clutter." The idea was to place advertisers as far away as they could from the religious shows that no one watched. But even back then Pat Robertson didn't take kindly to even a hint of second-class status. If Pat Robertson was going to go commercial he wanted to attract the big boys, the Coca-Colas, the bread companies, national advertisers with family-oriented kinds of products that evangelical Christians used as much as anybody else. Of course, like most UHF stations, CBN's first bread-and-butter sponsors were local mom-and-pop establishments. Even when a national advertiser came CBN's way, it wasn't necessarily a match. When a salesman at one CBN affiliate hooked his first big fish, a brand-name wristwatch manufacturer, he had to throw it right back. Turns out the wristwatch company had some spots done up to hawk its popular zodiac watches. "That episode pointed out that who we were and who they were, were two really different things," a former CBN station manager recalled. "Because when they sent us the commercials they really had no idea that zodiac watches might be difficult for us to put on our station. We ended up not being able to run the spots. We couldn't put horoscope spots on our network because that was occult. In those days you were constantly faced with those kinds of decisions." Although CBN was running ads, it was still a nonprofit and couldn't risk offending the evangelical Christians who supported it with donations. CBN was trying to coexist in two different worlds. Robertson knew that Christian programming alone couldn't hope to draw the audiences that commercial stations were accustomed to, so he set about developing a programming hybrid. "What Pat was interested in was to develop much stronger, broader audiences for the purposes of evangelism," one insider explained. "He felt the more sinners you got watching the program, the better opportunity you had to evangelize. So the original thought was to develop larger audiences, that Christian television in itself will not bring in those larger audiences, so we need to pepper the station with other programming, sitcoms and so forth, to get the audience we want to speak to." Today's *700 Club* is preceded by a rerun of *Name That Tune*. It's followed by FIT-TV, a half-hour fragment of the workout channel startup that Jake Steinfeld has been running for IFE at loss over the past couple years. The pneumatic Steinfeld leads buxom, Spandex-clad young women through an aerobic routine at some sunny Los Angeles locale. In the early days, programming for CBN was a real art: "At the time we had *Ironsides, Gilligan's Island,* Bugs Bunny," said one former CBN exec. "These were all syndicated product that worked. But what you had to know in terms of programming was not just that *Gilligan's Island* would work but where it would work best, at 2:30 or at 3. Because the audience you'd get at 3 with Bugs Bunny might be much better than with *Gilligan's Island.* So you really had to understand that marketplace and do research in that marketplace to find out what time the kids came home, when you start transitioning an audience. At CBN it was somewhat that, but you couldn't build the same kind of flow you have in commercial television because in your prime time you had your Christian programming, which is harder to build program flow with than it is with your sitcoms, because there's known factors with your sitcoms and your other types of programs." It's hard to know exactly what qualifications a program must have in order to earn the honor of running before or after *The 700 Club.* These days, at 11 in the evening, right after the rebroadcast of the same morning's *700 Club,* The Family Channel airs an hour of Three Stooges reruns.

CHAPTER SEVEN

The Club

I t is not terribly unusual for self-made moguls to attribute an unbroken string of career triumphs to God's will. Unbridled success naturally has its way of convincing a fair number of its recipients that some force, other than their own abilities and luck, is responsible for their favorable lot.

During the Pennsylvania miners' strike of 1902, railroad magnate George Baer wrote an open letter to the press in which he declared: "The rights and interests of the laboring man will be protected and cared for, not by the labor agitators, but by the Christian men to whom God in His infinite wisdom has given control of the property interests of the country."

Having outpaced and, therefore, having relieved so many others of their potential opportunities in some cases generates a sense of guilt that religious faith no doubt helps assuage. "I think religion is the most important thing in the world," Tom Monaghan, multimillionaire founder of the Domino's Pizza chain and a conservative Catholic, declaimed more recently. "It gives you a pretty clear guide on how to behave. . . . We're not here to squeeze as much pleasure into life as possible; what we do here determines where we spend the hereafter."

A 1995 poll commissioned by *U.S. News & World Report* and UCLA even found that 72 percent of Hollywood's decision makers believed in God.

On the other hand, a dearth of religious faith need hardly be looked upon as a hindrance to attaining great wealth and influence. Bill Gates—technological visionary, founder and CEO of Microsoft, and world-class billionaire—was asked by a reporter a few years ago if he, like Albert Einstein, had become aware of God through his exploration of the universe. He responded: "Well, Einstein may have believed in God but it didn't help him any. I mean, look at his work. . . . No, I don't regard myself as a particularly religious sort of person."

The official story of the Christian Broadcasting Network, the seed of Pat Robertson's corporate tree, not surprisingly, falls into the "God's will" category.

Having graduated magna cum laude from Washington and Lee University, reported for active duty in the Marine Corps during the Korean War, and attended Yale Law School, Pat Robertson circa 1955 had a résumé comparable to that of any promising young executive.

In 1953, he spent his summer in Washington working for the Senate Appropriations Committee. The summer after, he logged time in the New York office of W. R. Grace & Co., a conglomerate with worldwide interests in chemical production, banking, and manufacturing, as an intern to the tax counsel.

In most accounts, Robertson has portrayed his twentysomething self as a sociable bon vivant—"a swinger," in born-again parlance—who enjoyed drinking whiskey and playing poker as much if not more than studying. But like most young college graduates, Pat Robertson was looking for a sure shot at fleet financial success.

While at Yale, Robertson met a stylish, attractive young nursing student with auburn hair at a dorm open house named Adelia "Dede" Elmer, whom he married on August 27, 1954. Raised Catholic in a well-to-do Columbus, Ohio, family, Dede was a former Ohio State sorority sister and homecoming queen. Their wedding was sudden and secret—it took place ten weeks before the birth of Timothy, the couple's first child.

After Yale, Pat Robertson flunked the New York Bar exam. The failure was a psychological setback for a senator's son who had been preened his whole early life to become a member of the ruling class.

While his new wife finished her degree at Yale, Robertson took a management-training position offered by W. R. Grace. Almost immediately, Grace sent him to South America. Despite his lack of experience, Robertson was assigned to analyze textile plants in Peru and cement plants in Bolivia. A quick study, the young executive soon picked up the basics of management, accounting, and international finance. The opportunity gave Robertson invaluable firsthand experience of an American corporation operating overseas.

In John Donovan's authorized biography *Pat Robertson,* Robertson claimed that, even at the time, he viewed a prosperous American company reaping untold profits amid such dire poverty as unbefitting.

Although the Robertsons lived in a chauffeur's cottage on an estate in Staten Island overlooking New York Harbor, famously decorated with modish furniture and a Modigliani nude, money was a growing concern. By the end of 1955, Dede Robertson was pregnant with the couple's second child. Although by most accounts Pat Robertson was on the corporate fast track, he became restless with its strictures.

"There seemed to be a certain futility in it," he later told Donovan. "I was thinking, 'Well, I'll just make my fortune myself.'" Robertson saw little point in slaving away for decades, even at a potential $100,000 a year, in the name of benefiting stockholders. "If there was a chance of real money and if I was going to be successful, I'd rather do it my way than take a salary," he said.

In this vein, Robertson resigned from W. R. Grace after nine months and tried his entrepreneurial hand. In 1955, he and two fellow classmates from Yale Law founded Curry Sound Corporation, an electronic components concern, with $6,000 in borrowed funds (of which Robertson contributed $2,000). The 1957–1958 Manhattan telephone directory lists the firm's address as 308 West 30th Street.

Curry's chances for success rode on the development of a collapsible electrostatic loudspeaker. The partners hoped that the speaker could be built into airplanes and anywhere else sound was needed. But the speakers demanded a whopping thousand volts, an engineering glitch only expensive additional research would solve. As prospects for the product's profitability dimmed, so did Robertson's hopes for a financial windfall.

With a growing family to support, and debts mounting from the failing startup, Pat Robertson had no choice but to accept financial support from his parents.

Despite an exceptional education and pedigree, the 25-year-old Pat Robertson was on the verge of ruin.

———◄◦►———

It was Gladys Robertson who first led her youngest son to religion as a professional calling. Mrs. Robertson donated to a variety of fundamentalist evangelists, and when her son communicated to her his distraught state she arranged for him to have dinner with one of her beneficiaries, a Dutch immigrant named Cornelius Vanderbreggen.

The meeting with Vanderbreggen tripped off Robertson's spiritual rebirth. The well-dressed Vanderbreggen entertained Robertson at a swank Philadelphia restaurant where, in the middle of the meal (and much to Robertson's embarrassment), he foisted religious pamphlets on the formally attired waiters.

Vanderbreggen told Robertson, "You are the Lord's guest. God is generous, not stingy. He wants you to have the best. Order anything you want," according to Robertson's account from his 1972 autobiography, *Shout It From the Housetops* (written with Jamie Buckingham).

The notion of a personal relationship with Jesus as some kind of ultimate credential resonated deeply with the status-conscious Robertson. Until then "I thought God's people wore shabby clothes, baggy trousers, and suit coats that didn't match," he later wrote. "I thought they ate hamburger and boiled turnips." Vanderbreggen, to the contrary, had a tanned face and tipped big.

Within weeks, Robertson was off to Campus in the Woods, a Christian summer camp in Lake of Bays, Canada, leaving his seven-months pregnant wife behind.

Upon his return to New York, he enrolled at New York Theological Seminary.

The next few years were filled with spiritual awakening. The Robertsons moved from Staten Island to a two-bedroom apartment in Queens near the Bayside Community Methodist Church where Pat Robertson became the assistant pastor.

Robertson and a group of other seminary students began a quest, under the aegis of a magnetic pastor named Harald Bredesen, in pursuit of the Holy Spirit. Robertson was rebaptized by Bredesen and, like others in the group, soon found himself speaking in tongues. (He later recalled his first outburst, which instantly cured his son Timothy of a deathly fever, being in an "African dialect.")

Robertson's wholehearted embrace of the "charismatic" faith, a term later coined to describe those moved to spontaneous ululations by the Holy Spirit, would brand him for life. Regardless of his hallowed roots or future achievements, Pat Robertson's religious proclivities would from this point on prevent many from perceiving him as anything other than a religious zealot.

Originally a small offshoot of the twentieth-century American Pentecostal movement, charismatic evangelical Christianity underwent a period of renewal and growth during the early 1960s. The Pentecostals of the early 1900s were a loosely grouped set of Bible literalists, mostly rural poor folk in the South, who believed that speaking in tongues, prophesying, healing, and miracles were evidence of baptism by the Holy Spirit.

This fringe movement remained largely apart from the conservative evangelical establishment until after World War II when a movement of dynamic interdenominational Pentecostal healers, of whom Oral Roberts became the most well-known, began drawing audiences in the tens of thousands.

In 1960, Dennis Bennett, an Episcopalian priest in Van Nuys, California, announced publicly that he had spoken in tongues. The event was reported in mainstream media like *Time* magazine. Just a few years later, a group of young Catholic students at Notre Dame University reported speaking in tongues.

Meanwhile, the burgeoning healing movement had spawned prestige-oriented professional support organizations like the Full Gospel Business Men's Fellowship International (founded in Los Angeles by Demos Shakarian in 1954).

The revival's effect was a rapid mainstreaming of charismatic faith, to the extent that it became a main unifying force between virtually every Christian denomination in existence.

That Pat Robertson happened upon the charismatic movement in its earliest stages of revival turned out to be his luckiest of breaks.

According to David Edwin Harrell Jr., a professor at Auburn University and a Robertson biographer, "What Robertson tuned into was the one that was just going to boom. If you're a fundamentalist and your basic clientele is fundamentalist, there's a limit to how big you're ever going to get. Because there are just so many fundamentalists. And the secret of all those early media people was that if they had enough millions of people out there who liked their message, they could grow. Jerry Falwell momentarily made a big jump because of his political message, but Robertson from the beginning has been communicating with this very sizable group of people scattered into lots of different communities, Pentecostals, independent charismatics, charismatics within various denominations. In fact, in many ways he's one of the few foci where all of those people found common ground."

The following few years were cluttered with all-night prayer sessions, meetings with celebrity born-agains like Billy Graham and Mrs. Norman Vincent Peale, and religious retreats.

The chapter in *Shout It From the Housetops* in which Robertson recalls these experiences is titled "Drunk on New Wine" and describes rapturous communal spiritual gatherings that were—judging from the erratic behavior and beaded-sweat wisdom incurred—some sort of fifties-square equivalent of Grateful Dead concerts.

During the summer of 1957, Robertson's mother paid his family's way to the Word of Life Inn, a Christian camp in New York State's Adirondack Mountains.

In May 1959, Pat Robertson graduated from the seminary but couldn't find a position as a minister. His behavior became increasingly unpredictable as he allowed his faith to guide him.

One time when Dede went home to visit her family in Ohio, Robertson sold all their furniture and moved in with Dick Simmons, a friend from the seminary. The Simmons family were living in the ramshackle minister's residence of the Classan Avenue Presbyterian Church in the Bedford-Stuyvesant section of Brooklyn.

Living conditions in Bed-Stuy were squalid: The church was next door to a brothel; the manse was inhabited by assorted Jesus freaks, street people, and rats; and the young Robertson children (Timothy, Elizabeth, and Gordon) all shared one room. High-protein, low-cost soybeans were the main ingredient in most meals.

Pat Robertson had reached yet another dead end. Although he briefly entertained turning the neighborhood whorehouse into a mission, his wife was at her wits' end. When her mother visited, she begged Dede to return with the children to Ohio. Senator Robertson, originally pleased with his son's plan reprimanded his son for neglecting his familial responsibilities (in 1957, Willis Robertson had declared Pat and Dede dependents; Pat had earned $3,000 that year).

The Christian Broadcasting Network began unofficially in 1959 when Pat Robertson received word from his mother that a failing television station in Portsmouth, Virginia, was up for sale.

A pastor named George Lauderdale, a high school friend of Pat's, had been preaching in rural churches in the Lexington area and had happened upon a one-kilowatt UHF (ultra high frequency) station, Channel 27 in Portsmouth, Virginia, that was offering free air time for religious programming.

Lauderdale mentioned to Mrs. Robertson that the rundown station, owned by an automobile salesman named Tim Bright who used it as a tax deduction, was for sale. Lauderdale had appeared on the station with a gospel guitarist named Earl "Jigger" Jackson, but had no funds to purchase it.

Figuring that Pat Robertson, son of a senator, had ready money, Lauderdale told Bright that he had a friend who might be interested.

At first, Pat Robertson wasn't. He hardly had enough money to support his family in Brooklyn.

But he mulled over the possibility during the coming months. Although the asking price for the station was between $250,000 and $300,000, Robertson offered $37,000. That was $37,000 he didn't have.

Bright responded within a few weeks that he would accept $50,000 for the equipment and station or $25,000 for the equipment only.

Robertson took the fact that his bid was nearly in the middle of the two figures to be a sign from God that he must consider purchasing the station.

After months of soul searching back in Brooklyn (a time during which Dede Robertson also began speaking in tongues and became "born again"), Robertson came to a decision.

In the throes of this monumental personal crisis, Robertson took action in a manner that would define all his future endeavors: He walked into the Classan Avenue Church where he prayed and fasted for seven days.

At the end of the week, Robertson declared himself a changed man.

He experienced something of a political rebirth, as well. As a civilian in the 1950s, Robertson considered himself a liberal Democrat and had even run an Adlai Stevenson for President committee in New York.

"After my conversion to Christ my political outlook changed completely," he recalled to the *Virginian-Pilot* in 1968. "As it stands now, I'm not political in thinking but spiritual—except that I hope Bible-believing people will be placed in positions of political power."

The scriptures, he said, had commanded him to return home. So with $70 to their name, the Robertsons drove back to Virginia.

Without his father's assistance, Pat Robertson could never have gotten the Christian Broadcasting Network off the ground. In the final months of 1959, Senator Robertson provided his son with contacts, advice, even Christmas dinner: "[That year], we put the soybeans aside to eat a turkey provided by my parents," Pat Robertson later wrote.

And yet it was Pat Robertson's persistence alone that ultimately solidified his future. First, he cajoled Tim Bright into giving him a six-month option to buy the Portsmouth station for $37,000, with no cash up front. Then, he filed a charter with the State of Virginia to establish CBN as a nonprofit corporation (Robertson's major at Yale had been corporate law). Finally, he opened a commercial bank account for the station with a mere three-dollar donation from Jigger Jackson. As of January 11, 1960, Christian Broadcasting Network was official.

But matters were far from settled. The dilapidated old station had been pillaged by vandals; Bright was $44,000 in the hole with RCA; besides, the future of UHF television was sketchy at best. But Robertson labored on.

Most accounts (including his own) of this difficult middle period of Pat Robertson's life putter along in suitably awestruck fashion, dutifully making note of how at each trying and seemingly impossible juncture Robertson's prayers were answered and a miraculous solution was produced from on high.

When Robertson needed a job to support his family while getting CBN started, an old friend of the Robertsons gave him a ministerial post in Norfolk. When he tried to register the TV station with the Federal Communications Commission (FCC) under the call letters WTFC (as in "Television for Christ") but found they were already assigned, he dubbed it WYAH (as in "Yahweh," the Hebrew name for God). Even the actions of a potential investor who backed out after realizing that Robertson had no intention of getting his approval for operational costs were deemed provident.

"God wants this station to run on prayer," Dede Robertson told her husband to reassure him.

Although Robertson ascribes all fortuitous events from this era to divine guidance, lay observers might be pardoned for giving Robertson, who quickly proved himself to be an astute businessman with a knack for making something out of practically nothing, most of the credit.

In the coming months alone, Pat Robertson convinced RCA to erase much of the $44,000 debt, assembled a five-person CBN board of directors (which included himself, Dede, George Lauderdale, Harald Bredesen, and pioneering charismatic Bob Walker), and became the first person to apply for an FCC license for a TV station planning to devote 50 percent or more of its schedule to religious programming.

It wouldn't be the last time Pat Robertson would find himself ahead of the game.

Even then, Robertson himself was aware of the uniqueness of his vision. "As I began applying myself to my new job as Minister of Education at the Freemason Street Baptist Church [in Norfolk], I slowly realized my entire concept of the ministry had changed," he later recalled. Comparing himself to the Apostle Paul, who supported himself as a tentmaker so that he could preach, a religious man who held a secular job in order to minister to a congregation that couldn't afford to pay him, Robertson wondered: "Now I found myself in a reverse role. I was working at a church to support myself so I could minister through the television."

On October 1, 1961, at 3 o'clock in the afternoon, the Christian Broadcasting Network went on the air for the first time. Anyone in

Portsmouth, Virginia, who happened to be watching Channel 27 at that very moment would have seen a shaky black-and-white image of Pat Robertson, standing in front of a cardboard cross, praying. WYAH remained on the air—singers and preachers were the main on-air personalities—for the next two and a half hours.

It was the first time Pat Robertson had ever appeared on TV.

—◁◦▷—

At the start, CBN had only one camera. Virtually all the shows were broadcast live. Oftentimes, the back-to-back programming schedule required the camera operator to pan around a studio cluttered with stage sets in order for the next show to begin.

"Just hang on a minute, folks," the announcer, a young Ohio State broadcasting graduate named Neil Eskelin would say, as viewers received a vertiginous whirl around the room.

Live television posed a unique challenge for the young religious programmer. CBN's early offerings—dry liturgical renditions from dull, inexperienced religious performers, coupled with a novice technical staff—gave Robertson particularly strong incentive to develop original programming and to take risks of all kinds.

One of the first, *Mr. Pingo and His Pals,* a religious show for children, featured a teddy bear (Mr. Pingo) and Neil Eskelin as Cousin Neil, his ukulele-strumming pal. To liven up the show, Mr. Pingo would go scuba-diving (get held behind a fishbowl) or fly to the moon (made out of papier-mâché).

Pat Robertson's debut as a host was on a program called *Tomorrow's Lesson,* essentially a televised Sunday school class broadcast each Saturday night.

And so, from seven to ten each night, CBN went on the air, broadcasting any religious programming they could get their hands on, regardless of denomination: Half-hour shows produced by Billy Graham, Oral Roberts, and Kathryn Kuhlman were used simply to fill up empty slots.

But while the dearth of quality programming remained a large problem for the early CBN, financial insolvency became a much more urgent concern. Pat Robertson's first idea was to form an advisory board of wealthy area businessmen, and with this in mind, he initiated a series of breakfast meetings at a local hotel. Contacts made through Full Gospel Business Men's conferences in Washington provided more potential fund sources, though none ultimately panned out.

To make matters worse, the Freemason Street Baptist Church forced Robertson to choose between his minister's position and his fledgling TV station. He chose the latter.

Fortunately, within days, the nearby Parkview Baptist Church offered him his same $100-per-week salary but with fewer obligations, on a temporary basis. Six months later, however, Parkview hired a full-time pastor and terminated Robertson.

Before leaving, in a fit of ingenuity under pressure that would typify his later work, the distraught Robertson asked the church if he could use their mailing list to distribute a fund-raising letter for his TV station.

One of those letters reached Fred Beasley, a local ice and coal magnate. Beasley immediately offered Robertson a salary and a rent-free house near the Portsmouth station; and two years later, use of an estate on the grounds of Frederick College in Norfolk, which Beasley helped found.

In another stroke of good fortune, Congress passed a bill requiring that all televisions made after April 1964 be equipped with UHF capability.

Still, CBN required continual operating revenue. Pressure grew within the organization for Robertson to begin accepting commercials. Contributions from viewers hadn't kept pace with the costs of running an expanding TV network.

But Robertson was adamant about remaining commercial-free. Instead, he devised an incentive program he called "faith partners," whereby CBN viewers would "add their faith to ours," by pledging funds to the station.

In the fall of 1963, Pat Robertson broadcast CBN's first telethon (the first telethon ever had run only a decade earlier, in 1952, to raise money to send American athletes to the Helsinki Olympics). Estimating the station's monthly budget at $7,000, he beseeched his viewers to believe that 700 viewers would offer up ten dollars a month to keep the station running. He dubbed the telethon *The 700 Club*. By the week's end, CBN had monthly pledges totaling $3,500, only half of what Robertson had asked for, but enough to confirm the technique's effectiveness.

———◄○►———

By 1965, CBN had achieved some level of respectability. WXRI-FM was now the Virginia Tidewater region's number one radio station, thanks to a brand-new RCA 50,000-watt transmitter, paid for by $10,000 in donations solicited by Pat Robertson on the air in 1963.

Robertson had also hired Jay Arlan, a former ABC announcer and a Billy Graham radio programming director from North Carolina, who brought a much-needed professionalism to CBN.

But Robertson's biggest financial coup was the hiring of Jim Bakker. In Bakker, Robertson found his first genuine on-air celebrity.

Bakker, 25, was a former rock and roll disc jockey with a relaxed on-air presence. Together with his pixieish 23-year-old wife Tammy, Bakker devised a children's show featuring puppets for CBN called *Come on Over* (and later, *The Jim & Tammy Show*), which made its debut in September of 1965.

But it was Jim Bakker's abilities as a personality and shameless fund-raiser that made him so valuable. On the final evening of the 1965 telethon, at 11:00 P.M. on a Sunday, Bakker went before the camera and said: "Our entire purpose has been to serve the Lord Jesus Christ through radio and television. But we've fallen short. We need almost $10,000 a month to stay on the air, and we're far short of that. Frankly we're on the verge of bankruptcy and just don't have enough money to pay our bills. . . ." Then he began weeping.

Caught off guard, Robertson nonetheless quickly instructed the cameraman to keep his lens focused on the tears rushing down Bakker's cheeks.

CBN remained on the air till 2:30 in the morning as the phones kept ringing. The 1965 telethon was the first to bring in more than the projected $10,000 per month in operating costs.

———◦———

In 1966, Bakker prodded Robertson into letting him combine the call-in aspect of the telethons with a talk show format inspired by Johnny Carson's *Tonight Show*. Robertson was skeptical but gave his okay, insisting only that the show be called *The 700 Club Program*.

The format caught on almost immediately. Viewers soon began calling to demand the new program style as well as to make contribution. Robertson knew a good thing when he saw it and quickly dubbed himself the show's cohost.

No longer was traditional religious TV programming like preaching and singing the focus of CBN's schedule. With the advent of *The 700 Club*, Pat Robertson could claim for himself the potential audience sought after by any other television broadcaster.

Although Robertson and Bakker, as well as many other CBN employees, were practicing charismatics, "gifts of the spirit" like speaking in tongues were never displayed while on the air. Instead, guests from all walks of life were trotted onstage to relate their miraculous stories of healing and rebirth.

The 700 Club soon became so successful that CBN was able to finance the construction of a new multimillion-dollar waterfront headquarters in Portsmouth in 1967.

By mid-1968, the station warranted major attention in a 12-page supplement to the Norfolk *Virginian-Pilot:* "The control room complex of the renovated station carries a $400,000 price tag. The overall cost of the expansion has averaged about $11.25 per square foot. . . . About 26,000 pounds of re-bar steel are under the studio alone. . . . The lobby is hand-rubbed oak, specially matched and stained. . . . A magnificent mural, "Triumph of the Armageddon," . . . was constructed in squares of two feet each—the stones embedded in plaster of Paris and mounted on the wall."

What is most remarkable, however, about the local coverage of CBN at the time was how comfortably the network already fit in with the preexisting corporate and media landscape. Indeed, CBN's white-arched waterfront headquarters at 1318 Spratley Street looked more like something out of Walt Disney's Tomorrowland than a center for religious activity.

———◇———

As CBN grew, so did its influence both within and outside of conservative Christian circles.

Local Tidewater merchants and churches began buying thirty-minute time slots and received on-air recognition in return. And Pat Robertson's name became synonymous with homespun Christian national unity, in large part due to CBN's late-1960s schedule (6:00 P.M. to 11:00 P.M., Monday through Saturday; 1:00 P.M. to 6:00 P.M. on Sundays), which included the programs of other TV ministers, like Jerry Falwell, Rex Humbard, and Billy Graham, as well as *The 700 Club*.

Energetic and willing to experiment, Robertson cast himself as the preeminent innovator in Christian broadcasting. The *700 Club*'s endless stream of celebrity and everyday guests drew an increasingly far-flung audience. Always eager to infuse his broadcast with dramatic punch, Robertson frequently stumbled upon new and untried formats, such as call-in shows, today a talk-TV staple, but a *700 Club* feature since 1968.

Around the same time, Robertson met a young man named Scott Ross at a Full Gospel Business Men's conference. Ross, a former rock and roll DJ from Long Island who Robertson later described as "a long-haired, mustached man . . . dressed in a wild psychedelic shirt with tight pants and boots," had emceed concerts for the Beatles and the Rolling Stones and indulged in the "heavy drug culture."

Robertson soon hired Ross to draw adolescents to CBN. One of Ross's brainstorms was to bring a local Virginia Beach rock band into the studio. As the long-haired musicians played, the camera would focus on their dour expressions and Ross would interject comments such as: "Does God love these people?"

Ross and his wife, a former member of the Ronettes named Nedra Tally, eventually left Portsmouth after local church residents objected to their interracial marriage (Tally was black) and Ross's use of loud rock music in a religious setting.

By 1969, Pat Robertson's media empire consisted of the Portsmouth television station, a five-station radio network in upstate New York called CBN Northeast, a radio station in Bogotá, Colombia, and a television permit in Atlanta. To acquire the Bogotá station, called

Nuevo Continente, Robertson flew to South America, bargained the price down from $53,000 to $25,000, and then returned to Virginia and raised the necessary funds over the air after the fact.

Emboldened by his burgeoning success in the fund-raising realm, Robertson went so far as to tote up a list of other available media properties he might own: a TV station in Boston, a radio station in Costa Rica, WOR radio in New York, a news post in Israel. For $42 million, he estimated, he could have it all.

This rash of proposed acquisitiveness allowed Robertson to be duped for a series of months in 1970 by a woman claiming to be nurse and heir to the recently deceased widow of the Texas billionaire H. L. Hunt who had offered CBN $100 million in donations.

In addition to the spiritual lesson Robertson professed to have gained from the experience, he also obtained a valuable primer in hard business realities. Was CBN a ministry or a television station?

Although CBN's viewership figures continued to rise, Robertson found it increasingly difficult to sustain the Virginia flagship while growing a second station in Atlanta. Plus, as the host of a live daily talk show, Robertson could hardly be in two places at once. At the time, only the major networks could afford to "feed" programs to their affiliates through telephone lines.

This crippling dilemma bred yet more innovation. Robertson proposed packaging four-hour segments of CBN's original programming (principally *The 700 Club*) on videotape for syndication. In 1971 he hired advertising executive Stan Ditchfield to help him purchase time for CBN on commercial networks around the country, thus giving *The 700 Club* its first shot at nationwide exposure and nearly tripling CBN's fund-raising base.

The strategy paid off handsomely over the next few years as the country slipped into the recession of the mid-1970s. Languishing UHF stations turned to CBN, which was offering to purchase four hours of programming and then stage a telethon every few months; the independent station would be paid out of the proceeds.

In 1972, *The 700 Club* took on its first nonreligious affiliate in Charlotte, North Carolina. A young station owner based in Atlanta had been losing money in the Charlotte market and decided to take up Robertson's offer. His name was Ted Turner.

Jim Bakker, whose flamboyant manner and lifestyle were increasingly at odds with Robertson's more subdued, intellectual style, used the opportunity to begin planning his own network, having befriended Turner's program director in Charlotte.

Meanwhile Turner, angered by Robertson's attempt to solicit local advertising for his own fledgling station in Atlanta, threatened to pull the plug on Robertson in Charlotte. Turner soon agreed to replace Robertson's programming with similar religious fare produced by the Bakkers and the Charlotte program director. Both the Bakker program and Turner's Charlotte endeavor eventually failed. From there, the Bakkers joined forces with conservative California broadcaster Paul Crouch to form the Trinity Broadcasting Network, then, in 1974, returned to Charlotte to begin their own PTL (Praise the Lord) network.

Turner would later express deep regret about having unwittingly fostered both Robertson and Jim Bakker into TV's mainstream.

With the departure of Jim and Tammy Bakker CBN was depleted of two of its most magnetic celebrities, as well as an especially rich source of revenue.

Years later, Robertson disavowed his close relationship with the Bakkers. In 1987, Jim Bakker publicly admitted to an extramarital affair with church secretary Jessica Hahn. He was later convicted of bilking the PTL empire for millions of dollars of nonprofit funds—to fund a lavish lifestyle—and served jail time. Robertson, as presidential hopeful, claimed to have reprimanded the Bakkers for similar financial improprieties at CBN in 1972, just before they departed, although paperwork that would have verified those claims never materialized. Fund-raising and programming techniques devised by the Bakkers that Robertson made his own went unacknowledged.

"They really feel they deserve credit for *The 700 Club* format," said Mel White, who ghostwrote Robertson's book *America's Dates With Destiny* and who has interviewed the Bakkers about Robertson. "When you look back at Jim and Tammy's show, they had very different personalities from Pat, but the genre they were creating was very similar to Pat's genre today—only Mrs. Robertson isn't there and Pat never breaks into song."

Meanwhile, CBN had been adding affiliates across the country: By 1973, *The 700 Club* could be seen in Baltimore, Chicago, Houston, Philadelphia, Louisville, as well as on stations in California and Florida.

In 1972 Robertson approached Jerry Rose, today president of WCFC, an independent Christian television station in Chicago, to head up a commercial-free station he was starting in Dallas, Texas.

Rose had been a preministerial student in college but, like Robertson, understood that television was the wave of the future for the church.

Unlike Robertson, however, Rose decided to try his luck in secular commercial television and for the next 11 years worked as a director and producer for a Doubleday-owned station in Dallas and then a CBS affiliate in El Paso.

"From there, I was looking at the possibility of either staying commercial television or doing something in the Christian world, and had considered both very seriously and one day got a call from Pat Robertson," Rose recalled.

Not only did Rose agree to take the helm in Dallas but did Robertson one better.

"I knew that Doubleday wanted to do something with their commercial station there," said Rose, so he acted as a liaison between the owner of Doubleday and Robertson. Six months later CBN had taken over the commercial Channel 39.

"Prior to that, it was very difficult to find anything really meaningful in Christian television, even with Pat's stations," explained Rose. "At the beginning, his stations weren't very sophisticated at all.

"About the time that I went to Dallas, it had really begun to explode on the scene. It was right after that, that there was a greater explosion of Christian broadcasting: The National Religious Broadcasters really began to expand."

As general manager, Rose was not only in charge of running the Dallas station but also of repairing the decrepit facility. "CBN was committed to Dallas and so they were willing to put in enough money, but with that facility, I was not about to go in there and spend an awful lot of money, because that facility wasn't worth the investment,"

Rose said. But commitment bred ingenuity: "Quite frankly, what I did was I went to the salvage company and bought paneling that would look good and we went in and repainted and mainly cleaned the place up, and made as much investment in it as we needed to make in order to have a place that we felt comfortable asking people to come in."

Rose characterized Robertson as a big brother figure, and someone who was "better at television than a lot of the people I knew in commercial television—more savvy in terms of program development."

But by 1973, CBN's expansion was taxing Robertson's resources. "I felt like I was playing soccer and everyone else was playing football," he told *Channels* magazine, years later. "I'm a pragmatic person. When I see the facts, I react accordingly, rather than dealing in sentiment."

The Christian Broadcasting Network, Robertson concluded, was most definitely a TV station. And so, in 1973, CBN began replacing much of its religious programming with Hollywood reruns.

No longer saddled with its mandate to primarily broadcast relatively unpopular religious fare, ratings rose 400 percent almost immediately.

In 1976, *The 700 Club* could be seen on fifty stations in 25 out of the 30 largest metropolitan television markets in the nation. By 1978, the number of stations had grown to 150, plus an additional 35 overseas.

By rejiggering *The 700 Club*'s format in 1974, Pat Robertson seemed to acknowledge that if he was going to become a daily television presence in sophisticated, big-league markets like New York, San Francisco, and Los Angeles, his prime celebrity vehicle would also have to reflect the change in venue.

The 700 Club circa 1976 found Robertson sitting behind a desk, looking more than a little like Johnny Carson; Ben Kinchlow, a former black Muslim, Methodist minister, and CBN chauffeur, played Robertson's Ed McMahon. Also like Carson, Robertson had a row of chairs for his guests—even a live orchestra. Except, as Dick Dabney wrote in *Harper's*, "this one [was] scruffy, puffy-faced, and poor-looking, and given to chartreuse colors and rhinestones, with a chubby leader whose prime function seemed to be that of taking mirthful abuse from Robertson. Maybe it was 'Christian' abuse, too, in that it wasn't risqué; but there was a hum of *The Tonight Show* vibes to it—the poised, hip king reigned by subtle abuse, and representing in his transcendent self a golden mean between tight-assed parochialism on the one hand and bohemian whoopee on the other."

———◦———

As the amiable host of the most popular daily broadcast geared primarily toward American evangelical Christians, Pat Robertson drew an increasingly impressive array of celebrity and political guests.

By the mid-1970s, *The 700 Club* could count on regular appearances from a surprisingly far-flung group of born-again personalities—from singer B. J. Thomas to Dallas Cowboys coach Tom Landry to ex–Black Panther Eldridge Cleaver.

During this time, Robertson became increasingly bold about doing away with the traditional evangelical taboo against bringing politics into the religious realm. In 1974, for example, he lambasted President Nixon on the air, accusing the Watergate-logged chief executive of having pulled a "cruel hoax" on the American people.

And world-class political figures became a *700 Club* staple. Israeli prime minister Yitzhak Rabin visited the show, thanks in part to Robertson's staunch pro-Israel stance (Robertson believes that all Jews will return to Israel before the apocalyptic Second Coming). Jimmy Carter, whose status as a born-again Christian played a prominent role during his presidential campaign, appeared on the program soon after he was elected.

But although he and other television preachers had campaigned hard for Carter in 1976, Robertson later stated that Carter had deceived him. "I sensed something was wrong when I interviewed him for our show," Robertson told *Harper's*. "There was this wonderful exterior charm to him. But underneath, terrible coldness. It was frightening."

Carter was the last Democrat presidential candidate to receive Robertson's support.

In 1977, Ben Kinchlow joined *The 700 Club* as cohost. Kinchlow, a six-foot-four African-American from Texas, added a desperately needed minority quotient to the show. The former Muslim-turned-Methodist minister had been director of CBN's counseling center in Dallas, and first appeared on *The 700 Club* as guest. A folksy but sincere born-again version of Bryant Gumbel, Kinchlow helped usher in the show's modern era.

Still, the show was dull, by nonreligious programming standards. Robertson sat behind his desk the whole 90 minutes and, because there were only two or three guests per program, the interviews tended to run too long.

"The problem with CBN was not so much the equipment, it was the programming," recalled Gerard Straub, who joined the network as assistant director of network operations in 1978, was fired for an adulterous affair in 1980, and later wrote a book called *Salvation for Sale* chronicling his experiences. "The problem was what it said, how it said it, and how it presented those ideas."

While at CBN, Straub witnessed what he called a "flourish of creativity" at *The 700 Club,* where suddenly the quality of equipment the network could afford matched the ambitions of the production staff.

Like many other CBN employees of that era, Straub had little experience running a TV operation. Although he had chalked up years at one of the major networks in New York, it was in a noncreative position, as a midlevel operations manager.

In anticipation of a move to spacious new digs in Virginia Beach, Virginia, Robertson and CBN were eager to extend the network's programming beyond *The 700 Club.* Among the new shows, most short-lived, were *USa.m.,* an early-morning talk show, and *Another Life,* which billed itself as the first Christian soap opera. Although 875 episodes of *Another Life* eventually ran between 1981 and 1984, CBN never generated ad revenues sufficient to justify its exorbitant production costs.

During one planning meeting, Straub encouraged Robertson to shorten *The 700 Club* to an hour, reasoning a condensed format would enliven the broadcast. Robertson and the others present immediately refused. Soon after, though, Robertson promoted Straub to producer of *The 700 Club.*

"I felt it was to his credit that he recognized that I had some truth, that I was looking at it a little differently from everybody else," said

Straub. "He knew that the show was boring, he just didn't know what to do about it, and he didn't have anyone to talk to about it. As long as the cameras got turned on, and the lights were on, and everything looked fine, the rest was up to him. And so he was carrying this tremendous burden that no person can really do."

Soon Robertson's desk was removed, the furniture was upgraded, and the *700 Club* set began looking more like a living space than a talk-show set. "We introduced theme shows," Straub said. "If, for instance, I had an astronaut on, I created a moonscape set. If I had an economist on, I remember creating a gigantic dollar bill." When David Wilkerson, the evangelist and coauthor of the best-selling ghetto drama *The Cross and the Switchblade* showed up, he found himself being interviewed by Robertson on a set designed to look like a New York City street. Admitted Straub, "I was out of control."

Because funds were not always available to create the hours of original programming, new shows would frequently be concocted out of thin air. *The Lesson* was a half-hour show that featured Robertson in front of a blackboard teaching a Bible lesson. *The Ross Bagley Show* starred the DJ from a local CBN radio station narrating recycled music segments from *The 700 Club.*

"We were making shows out of nothing," Gerard Straub recalled. "We would just recycle crap and Robertson would sit in the studio for a half hour and do all these introductions and slap them together and *bingo:* Bagley was a popular show, Christians responded to it."

But the general willingness to try anything occasionally elicited bigger, more lasting results. "I recall saying once, Why don't we just take reruns of good old shows, which at that time you could get very cheaply, and then dump some of these second-rate preachers?" By 1981, CBN had abandoned virtually all religious programming other than *The 700 Club.* "We were doing Nickelodeon before anybody knew what Nickelodeon was," Straub observed.

Out of this lucrative formula, the Family Channel was later born.

———◁◦▷———

But even as the production values and sheer watchability of *The 700 Club* improved in the early 1980s, Robertson whittled down the range of topics covered. The nonexistence of separation of church and state language in the United States Constitution, the satanic properties of "secular humanist" or "communist" organizations such as the American Civil Liberties Union and the American Bar Association, and the systematic persecution of Christians in America's public square all became *700 Club* mantras.

"The ingenious thing about *The 700 Club*," said Robertson biographer David Edwin Harrell Jr., "is maintaining contact with all those people with very orthodox charismatic theological talk and then you would have cushioned in that lectures on supply-side economics, the Sandinistas, and various other political topics."

Robertson observer and opponent Edmund Cohen was more sanguine: "What Robertson wants to do with *The 700 Club* is communicate radical positions to his hard-core followers, but maintain deniability regarding those hard-core positions with the rest of society."

Either way, Robertson made it his business to "educate" his *700 Club* viewers about a wide range of subjects that otherwise—that is, had they not emanated from their trusted host's lips—they would have expressed little interest in.

In 1982, for example, Robertson spent weeks on *The 700 Club* explaining to his viewers that Israel's invasion of Lebanon that year was detailed in the Bible. He claimed Israeli troops were fulfilling the Old Testament prophecy of Ezekiel, who spoke of an imminent war between Israel and the northern "land of Magog," which Robertson took to be the Soviet Union. The whole world will soon be "in flames," he prophesied, and God would come to Israel's aid and destroy the Soviet Union.

By the year 2000, Robertson predicted, Jesus Christ will have returned and fought a battle to the end with a dictatorial Antichrist—the Armageddon. Jews will see the light or be destroyed and the righteous (spirit-filled Christians) will prevail.

During one mid-eighties *700 Club* broadcast, Robertson told cohosts Ben Kinchlow and Danuta Soderman that he believed that "Christians and Jewish people" were the only ones capable of holding elected office in the United States.

"Obviously you're not saying that there are no other people qualified to be in government or whatever if they aren't Christians or Jews," Kinchlow responded, ably handing Robertson an on-air opportunity to clarify his statement.

But Kinchlow raised his eyebrows when he heard Robertson's answer: "Yeah, I'm saying that. I just said it. I believe it."

Logic would have it that the only way Robertson could ever achieve the level of mainstream credibility he so clearly desires would be to water down his radical religious beliefs. Yet on *The 700 Club,* he has rarely done so.

So while on one hand, he has continued to publicly express arch-conservative views far right enough to resemble at times the anarchical spoutings of white-supremacist militia groups, doing so has done little to hinder the growth of his mainstream reputation. It has been Pat Robertson's particular genius to juggle this abject kookiness with a distinct notion of quality and somehow keep both balls in the air. "If one watches *The 700 Club* today, there's never any effort to hide the radical charismatic beliefs," observed David Edwin Harrell.

According to Harrell, *The 700 Club* has always held a unique spot in religious broadcasting for a very clear-cut reason. "The major difference with Robertson was that, from the beginning, he didn't preach," Harrell said. "It was always a talk show. Now early on, the talk show didn't have any political content but then at some point he began to talk about both economics and politics. Frequently what led him into politics were his prophetic predilections, but then it more and more became simply a broader political platform."

Today *The 700 Club* appears three times a day on The Family Channel—at 10:00 A.M., 10:00 P.M., and 2:00 A.M. (all times are eastern standard). The 90-minute show is broadcast live in the morning and usually edited down to an hour for the late-night and early-morning repeats.

"Nobody in secular broadcasting logs up as many hours of on-camera live television as Pat Robertson," observed Cohen, a Robertson watchdog who monitors the show and supplies mainstream media sources with salient *700 Club* footage. "Having a daily show more than an hour long, the sheer number of hours of live television is just mind-boggling. There are so many hours of it that you can't sift through it after the fact. Only by keeping up with it every day and saving the few minutes that count, can one do the job. There is so much stuff, and the yield is too low."

CHAPTER EIGHT

---◇---

At the 1992 Republican National Convention, Houston, Texas, August 19, 1992

". . . A resident of Virginia Beach, Virginia, and the president of the Christian Broadcasting Network, *Mister* Pat Robertson!" It's 7:20 P.M. on August 19, 1992 at the Republican National Convention in Houston, Texas. And as a resonant baritone voice booms the above words over the loudspeaker system, Pat Robertson enters stage right and makes a diagonal beeline for the imposing classically fashioned gray rostrum at the center. But Pat Robertson does not walk quickly, or with any stiffness in his gait. Rather he shambles, shifting his full weight from one leg to another as his lets his head bob from side to side. A broad smile inches across his face as he nears his destination. In his left hand, he holds a sheaf of papers. As a gleeful roar rushes up from the convention floor, Pat Robertson takes his papers in both hands, places them on the stand in front of him, then props his arms on both ends of the dais and rests his full weight upon them. He is wearing a dark business suit, either brown or dark navy and a maroon foulard tie. On the floor, by the Virginia state banners, supporters fibrillate American-flag blue placards with the words "Knock 'Em Flat, Pat!!!" printed in white block letters. In order to allow for a few moments of unfettered hootin' and hollerin', Robertson licks his lips while scanning the room. His eyes squint up as he appears to effectively contain what might in other circumstances be a hearty guffaw. One thing's for sure: Robertson's mien is not the goo-goo-eyed, beatific glaze ordinarily associated with televangelists. The late comedian Jack Benny, it was often noted, could elicit laughter from an audience without uttering a single word, simply by giving just the right bemused look at the precise silent moment. On this occasion, Pat Robertson possesses a similar such impeccable timing. "Seventy-five years ago," he begins, "a plague descended upon the world and covered the nations of Eastern Europe like a dark cloud." Robertson's expression has changed midsentence. Suddenly, he appears not so much like the cosmopolitan bon vivant but more like a mad ship captain, braving nature's gale force from his prow. In case you hadn't already guessed, the "dark cloud" Robertson is talking about is Communism. Robertson says that over time Communism spread throughout the whole world, threatening its very existence. Right about now, on C-Span's live convention broadcast, Robertson is ID'ed as "Rev. Pat Robertson" in bright yellow type right across his double Windsor. The secularization of Pat Robertson never really stuck. During his 1988 run for the GOP nomination, Robertson publicly derided those who referred to him by his recently dropped honorific as religious bigots. The real reasoning behind it, other than simply to shield his agenda from the uninformed, is hard to imagine. "Ladies and gentlemen," Robertson continued, "it was Ronald Reagan, George Bush, and the Republican policies which brought communism to its knees." Another wave of cheers cascaded over Robertson. Just now a wide camera angle reveals the two wafer-thin glass TelePrompTer screens that bow at Robertson's sides, making him look for all the world like an Egyptian prince cosseted by palm fronds. Only a year earlier, in his book *The New World Order,* Robertson took Bush to task for his memberships in the Council on Foreign Relations and the Trilateral Commission, two organizations that, according to Robertson, are a continuation of a centuries-old conspiracy toward one-world government. "Indeed," wrote Robertson, "it may well be that men of goodwill like Woodrow Wilson, Jimmy Carter, and George Bush . . . are unknowingly and unwittingly carrying out the mission and mouthing the phrases of a tightly knit cabal whose goal is nothing less than a new world order for the human race under the domination of Lucifer and his followers." Robertson had become positively obsessed with the Bush administration's invocation of the phrase "new world order" to signify American growth and renewal. Those three words, he argued, conjured up notions of Adolf Hitler, the Freemasons, and that legendary demon anarchist—John Lennon, of course. But the convention in Houston was no time for dire and paranoid end-time fantasies. Pat Robertson lectured the minions primarily on the fall of communism, the importance of lower taxes and less government. "Lyndon Johnson called it the Great Society, Bill Clinton calls it the New Covenant," Robertson continued, "but, my friends, whatever name you call it, it's still the liberal welfare state, and we want no part of it." (That Senator A. Willis Robertson was a Woodrow Wilson protégé, a Freemason, and an early supporter of Franklin Roosevelt suggests that Pat Robertson would be a field day for Freudian scholars.) Pat Robertson talked about the crisis confronting the American family that night at the Astrodome, but not in the context one might think. The way he told it was that higher taxes, not social breakdown, were threatening wholesome American family values. Robertson said that, since 1940, the U.S. federal budget had increased from $13 billion to $1.5 trillion (an increase of 10,900 percent) even though the population of the United States had only increased from 130 million to 250 million (92 percent). (At this very moment, C-Span's camera cleverly panned the audience to show another grand manipulator of statistics, Rush Limbaugh, not paying attention.) Today, he added, the average family paid 25 percent of its income in federal taxes, as compared to 2 percent in 1950. Robertson criticized the Democrats for their spending habits: too much spent on endangered species research; too little spent on national defense; too much spent on "Great Society" entitlements. He even shot off a Reaganesque zinger every once in a while: "Come to think of it," he quipped, "Slick Willie talks like John Wayne but acts like Gomer Pyle." Furthermore, those "check-kiting Democrats in Congress" couldn't be trusted: Surely any sensible citizen would know better than to vote to elect a president who would endorse those crooks. It's just that virtually everything Robertson said in Houston sounded so damned *sensible*. The man is a master of what I'll call the backward verbal arabesque. Check out this sentence Robertson crafted to attack Bill Clinton: "He told *People* magazine that he wouldn't let his 13-year-old daughter get her ears pierced, but he wants to give your 13-year-old daughter the choice, without your consent, to destroy the life of her unborn baby." Let's try unraveling it. The buzzwords "unborn baby" are an obvious sop for hard-line pro-lifers, Robertson's natural constituency. Then there's a midsentence shell game where Robertson implies that the issue he's referring to is not actually abortion but rather granting grave, unalienable rights to young children. This twist thereby incorporates a slightly larger, broader-based group of conservatives who may not like the idea of abortion, but who like the idea of their children doing whatever they please behind their parents' backs even less. Move back to the bit about Bill Clinton not allowing his 13-year-old daughter Chelsea to get her ears pierced, and the Arkansas Democrat sounds like a plain old spoilsport. The reference to *People* magazine is an especially knowing touch. Depending on one's perspective, it gingerly implies either that Clinton is a bargain-basement "sell out" politician (note that both Robertson and Ralph Reed have been the subjects of their own *People* profiles) or that he is, at the very least, slight, scandalous, worthy of gossip, and eager to chat about the petty personal details of his home life. It's no wonder that in the months after Bill Clinton was elected president in November 1992, his reputation among conservative Republicans dipped below traditional levels of partisan distaste. "To many of them the president's character is not simply flawed, it's criminal," *Rolling Stone*'s Francis Wilkinson was writing by the end of 1994. "His election was not just a fluke, it was illegitimate." But as Pat Robertson reaches the final third of his speech, he lets his rightist freak flag fly ever so briefly. He claims Clinton wants to "appoint homosexuals to his administration," a definitively phony-sounding allegation, bred of pure bigotry and, of course, of utterly no consequence. That's why when Robertson follows it up by saying, "Since I have come to Houston, I have been asked repeatedly to define traditional values—I say very simply, to me and to most Republicans, traditional values begin with faith in Almighty God," it sounds oddly conciliatory. "Woooo! Wooo-woooo!!!" That's Ralph Reed, right after Robertson says the word *God*. Captured by a C-Span camera on the Astrodome floor. In his pinstripes. Waving a Robertson placard, both arms high over his head, and hooting like a preposterously spirited schoolboy at a football pep rally. Hooray for the home team. But for all his speech's harsh invectives, Pat Robertson reads the crowd's mood and gauges his expressions. Two gigantic video screens relay the nuances to the floor. When Robertson speaks of a "more benign but equally insidious plague" than Communism, he's talking about big government, and he hunches his shoulders and furrows his brow. But the delivery is different for each of Robertson's most memorable lines of the evening. When he utters the John Wayne–Gomer Pyle line, his lower lip twitches into a rascally smile. For a moment the dramatic tension subsides, and laughter breaks out as the camera pans a sea of outmoded haircuts and white faces. It gets ugly only when Robertson attacks Clinton personally: "When Bill Clinton talks about family values, I don't believe he is talking about families or values. He's talking about a radical plan to destroy the traditional family and transfer many of its functions to the federal government." But after he says this, Robertson takes an easy step back from the podium and eases his visage. The hooded eyebrows and vulture's gaze instantly morph into a cool, saturnine grin, crow's feet and all. With that, he deftly segues into a paean to the then-current First Lady, Barbara Bush, whose name he pronounces in the squishy-cute voice familiar to his television fans. Here is the first glimpse of the Pat Robertson, that most reassuring and mannerly of TV living-room guests. Barbara Bush is so gracious and dedicated and caring, he explains, and it sounds so reasonable that we agree. In 1985, Pat Robertson visited Sudan with Barbara Bush and her husband and saw the way she coddled a starving infant. It's significant to note that later that year, in the weeks of November after George Bush relinquished the presidency to Bill Clinton, that blame for the defeat was heaped upon the shoulders of another Pat—Pat Buchanan—who told the main assemblage one night before, that Hillary Clinton "believes that 12-year-olds should have a right to sue their parents, and she has compared marriage, as an institution, to slavery" and that, when it came to Vietnam, Bill Clinton "sat up in a dormitory in Oxford, England, and figured out how to dodge the draft." Robertson's attacks were certainly more viable than Buchanan's. In his speech, Pat Robertson claimed the Democrats in Congress sanctioned a $450,000 study to determine whether "students who do their homework learn more" and another for $350,000 that figured out that people eat more at a smorgasbord than ordering from a menu. In retrospect, Robertson's figures even sound believable, presumably because half a million dollars for a federal survey examining student work habits doesn't sound like a lot—unless you oppose public schools. In a forum where the loudest and most strident speaker makes the most political hay, Robertson's was a subtle victory. Subtle enough that he could comfortably go on *Larry King Live* mere days after Bush's '92 defeat and tell King that the religious right bore no responsibility for the Republican candidate's defeat. "Absolutely not one iota, Larry," Robertson said. "One line on abortion and two lines on homosexuality," he continued, "yet, my speech has been characterized as some flaming right-wing thing. It wasn't at all. It was a mainstream utterance." And, as in so many instances before, Pat Robertson was absolutely right. He had expressed himself appropriately at just the right moment. In his guise as steward to the Republican mainstreamers, Robertson was most gentlemanly and convincing. He had not used his bully pulpit to take issue with the citizenship's essential ungodliness. He also managed to tip off his diehard supporters. Words like "plague" and "New Covenant" (as in "We don't need a New Covenant. We need a new Congress!") are Armageddon talk, calculated to appeal to fundamentalist Christians geared up for the end times but generic enough to glide by those with more mainstream sensibilities. Even the phrase "One nation under God" takes on multiple meanings when parting from Pat Robertson's lips. Consider an interview British commentator David Frost did with Robertson on the eve of the 1988 election, during which the candidate clarified his positions on, among other things, Hurricane Gloria, the storm he heretofore claimed to have turned away from Virginia Beach in 1985. He was prepared to be laughed at by people all over the nation, he told Frost, and "I knew I could just as easily have kept my mouth shut and let the thing hit and not get involved." But he couldn't let that many people die. So he had led his *700 Club* viewers in prayers that whisked the hurricane "harmlessly out to sea" and up to Long Island, New York, where it killed six people and wrought $300 million in damages. "So it was, of course, a miracle. . . . There's no other explanation. The newspaper the next day said we were very lucky. Well, I don't think it was lucky. I think it was divine intervention." Those people on Long Island should have prayed, he said. Robertson swore he could not be held responsible for the hurricane once it left Virginia Beach.

CHAPTER NINE

The Coalition

On December 13, 1995, at ten minutes after 8 P.M., Ralph E. Reed Jr. stood up from a chair situated between two large potted ferns in the Oolie conference room at the Lautenberg Family Jewish Community Center (JCC) of Greater Morris in Whippany, New Jersey, and calmly walked stage right to one of two wood-grain podiums set atop the riser.

This brisk winter night, Reed was out in the cold, both literally and emblematically. If the 34-year-old executive director of the Christian Coalition was merely an obedient attack dog hired by Pat Robertson, as some had reputed, tonight his tether had been let out awfully long.

A broad-shouldered man with curly orange hair and glasses named David Twersky, the editor of the MetroWest Jewish News and the evening's moderator, had introduced Reed. After acknowledging "all of the tzimmes about tonight," Twersky proudly declared that the lecture, the fourth in a series titled "Jews, Politics, and the Moral High Ground," was Reed's "first visit with a grassroots Jewish community."

Reed wore a dark navy business suit, a starched white button-down oxford shirt, and a tie decorated with horizontal stripes of navy, maroon, and gold. A carefully folded white handkerchief tufted up from his left breast pocket.

Even in the harsh overhead lights, his lean cheeks and blue eyes sparkled bright in the bronze oval of Pan-Cake makeup that circled his face.

"My fax machine has been burning with such intensity over the last two weeks about all the controversy involving my being here," said Reed, "that I can't wait to hear what I have to say."

A nervous but gentle laughter rippled through the audience as the executive director of the Christian Coalition launched into his prepared speech.

Simon Jaffe, JCC MetroWest's executive director, later told me that the JCC approached Ralph Reed first, not the other way around. "Dr. Reed was being interviewed on National Public Radio back in May when he issued the Contract With the American Family," said Jaffe. "I became intrigued by who this person was and a number of the issues in regards to the contract and wondered in developing a speaker series for the fall if he might be somebody who would stimulate an interesting discussion."

———◇———

For those audience members prepared to witness the incoherent rantings of a fire-and-brimstone zealot, Reed's presentation came as something of a shock. Tall and handsome, Reed exuded a nearly deferential respect and easy rapport while addressing a constituency that had every reason, historically and ecumenically, to regard him with the utmost suspicion.

"Tonight I wish to speak frankly, openly, and honestly about an issue that confronts us and our communities and those that we strive to represent," Reed said, sounding only a little bit like a young man artificially deepening his voice to convey gravity. "It is the undeniable and palpable suspicion and, I do not overstate it to say fear, that divides the Christian community from many American Jews. We must confront the troubling reality that there were some who did not wish for me to be here tonight. Some which believe that the First Amendment does not extend always to evangelical Christians. And we must confront the troubling reality that 30 to 40 million evangelical Protestants and pro-family Catholics and their Greek Orthodox allies, probably one of the largest constituencies in the electorate today, are an object of fear and anxiety and suspicion in the Jewish community."

As he spoke, Reed occasionally sliced the air with his practiced right hand for emphasis. Stereotyping of religious conservatives and bigotry is being directed toward "those of us with faith in God," he intoned. Christians and Jews have a history of divisiveness, he said, but in today's America they have at least their notion of religiosity in common. His message, a declaration of the United States as a pluralistic society that "honors the role of religion and faith in our life," sounded remarkably mainstream, even oddly reassuring.

Only the vocal group of protesters weathering the brisk December air outside the modern building's front entrance (People for the American Way, the National Organization for Women, as well as various gay and lesbian groups all sent representatives to the demonstration) belied Reed's conciliatory claims.

That night Reed told one reporter that the protesters reminded him of all the minority hate groups of the American right that used to sustain themselves by making at least enough money to keep their staff employed but never moved the larger voting populace.

Ironically, early requests from the JCC for Reed as a speaker had been met with casual disregard. Reed's main condition upon accepting the invitation to speak was a refusal to share the podium with an opposition voice—Mark Stern of the American Jewish Congress and Anti-Defamation League director Abraham Foxman had been a few of the names suggested.

MetroWest's Simon Jaffe said that Reed demanded this exclusivity on the grounds that what made the gathering appealing was a chance to express the Christian Coalition's views in an uninterrupted and dramatic forum.

"This is new, and it's a smart tactic from their point of view," said Barbara Handman of People for the American Way, who attended Reed's Whippany engagement.

Of course, unlike the most prominent of his vocal opponents, Ralph Reed is a celebrity. Years of television appearances, mostly of the political roundtable sort, have purchased Reed the most Teflon-like finish American society has to offer: fame.

By capitalizing on this recently acquired currency as a genuine pundit, Reed had even been able to secure a similarly singular forum on *Meet the Press* the week earlier.

"They consider themselves of prime interest and we can be discarded," Handman lamented. "And in fact, I guess, that's true, because look at these two examples."

But when I asked Handman whether she thought a popular figure of the left with comparable cachet might try the same tactic given the same opportunity, she answered, "Probably."

———◦———

Ralph Reed is of course no stranger to controversy. Well before he was hired by Pat Robertson in 1988, at the age of 27, to lead the Christian Coalition, Reed had made his mark as a conservative firebrand, having espoused conservative Republican politics from his days as a student at the University of Georgia.

In a column for the school paper and as a member (and later, executive director) of a countrywide GOP student organization, the College Republican National Committee, he whetted an appetite for airing his provocative positions publicly.

This night was no exception. Reed trumpeted the fact that both houses of Congress were Republican for the first time in 40 years. The 1994 election alone resulted in a switch of 53 seats in the House and 8 seats in the Senate from Republican to Democrat. The number of Democrats in the House was down to 196, a figure that had not been so low since World War II. Seventy-two percent of all Americans live in states with Republican governors.

He also stated that nearly every candidate on the federal, state, and local level that had changed his or her party affiliation in the last year had gone from the Democratic to the Republican party. "So you can go on and on and see that we are likely—no matter what the result of the '96 presidential election—likely to have a Republican Congress for the foreseeable future," Reed said.

According to Reed, the tide was turning. And his constituency, conservative Christians, were at the forefront of the next wave. "We can agree or disagree on the issues," he said, awkwardly planting a stiffened hand into his pants pocket. "We can have fights, we can have disputes. That's legitimate, that's part of a pluralistic, free society. But I think what we cannot do is to demonize and to stereotype this constituency because the reality is, ladies and gentleman, that this constituency that I represent and that the Christian Coalition aspires to give voice to, is too large, it is too significant, and it is too diverse to be ignored and taken for granted by either political party."

Then Reed spouted the numbers—"and these are not my figures, these are a major television network's," he said. He claimed 33 percent of all voters who entered the voting booth in 1994 were either born-again evangelical Christians or pro-life Roman Catholics who attended church or Mass four times or more per month. Seventy percent of those voters were Republican; 24 percent, Democrat.

And yet more statistics: Forty percent of the Christian Coalition's membership live in the South, 12 percent in the Northeast, 24 percent in the Midwest and Mid-Atlantic, and 17 percent live in the West. About two-thirds are Protestant, about a third are Roman Catholic. Two percent of the Christian Coalition's membership is Jewish. Sixty-two percent of those voters are women. "And by the way, half of those women work outside the home," Reed glowered.

Sixty-six percent have either attended or graduated from college; 14 percent have graduate or professional degrees. They have an average household income of $40,000 a year, which is about a third above the national average. Seventy-six percent are married, 66 percent have children. Their median age is 44 years, "about two years above the natural average."

Reed boiled down all this data and more to the conclusion that the average member of his constituency was a woman in her mid-thirties to mid-forties with children who works outside the home.

The members of the Christian Coalition are by no means "poor, uneducated and easy to command," Reed asserted, repeating a phrase Michael Weisskopf of *The Washington Post* first used in 1992 to describe Robertson sympathizers, a phrase that has become the flock's battle cry ever since.

———◇———

Children, Israel, and religious tolerance: These were the three primary issues identified by Reed as the ground shared by his largely liberal Jewish audience and his own conservative Christian constituency.

"He certainly pushed all the right buttons," was the way it was put by one onlooker, a bulky middle-aged woman with gray, bristly hair and wire-rim glasses.

"When we surveyed religious conservative voters prior to the 1994 elections," Reed told the crowd. "Here's what we found: Their number one concern was the deficit and the economy; their number two concern was crime; and their number three concern was education. They're concerned about things like whether they can send their child to a school in their neighborhood. Whether or not that child is going to be able to read or write or add and subtract and be able to perform on standardized tests at a level equal to or exceeding their counterparts in other Western industrialized nations. They are concerned about whether or not they can send their nine-year-old to a playground three blocks from their home and whether or not that child is going to come home alive or not."

For a moment, the only sound in the room was the clicking keys of the notebook computers cradled in the laps of the reporters in a near corner.

Reed's comments on Israel were even blunter. "I want you to know that as a Christian Community that we will continue to stand with the nation of Israel, with the Israeli people, and with Jews all over the world in praying for and working for peace in that troubled region." When he mentioned a letter he had issued to Bob Dole, Newt Gingrich, and Bill Clinton urging the movement of Israel's capital from Tel Aviv to Jerusalem, he received his biggest applause of the evening.

"Listen, this is a guy who I think is one of the most sophisticated guys I've ever met," David Twersky, who described himself as a "right-wing Democrat but a leftist on Israel," told me later. "I think he's unbelievably sophisticated and that his biggest problem is Robertson." Twersky added that, in fact, Reed had been a moderating force in American Christian–Jewish relations in regard to Israel. Whereas the "so-called Christian Zionist crowd" had over the past supported Israel's conservative Likud party, lining up against U.S. troops in the Golan Heights and aid to the Palestinians, Reed had to stay out of the debate at the behest of the Israeli embassy.

"Now, every instinct in his being must want to line up with the Christian Zionists and the Likud," Twersky said. "But he didn't do it because he's playing a different game. He's separating, as Irving Howe once said, between the near and the far. And he's playing a near game. I think that's enormously important: that he showed toward the Jewish establishment the kind of maturity that one would want out of a player in deference to what the government of Israel wanted."

In an attempt to communicate his constituency's empathy for the audience's "boundless suffering," Reed acknowledged the tragic history of the Jews in the twentieth century. Here, he visibly lost the crowd.

"[History] cannot teach me," Reed said, "what your parents and what your grandparents have related to you: breathless accounts of hiding in attics and cellars to survive Easter Sunday pogroms in the old mother Russia and in eastern Europe. Of midnight escapes from the Gestapo. Of being forced to sew yellow stars on clothing or on a coat sleeve. And having epitaphs like 'Killer of Christ' hurled at you, occasionally by leaders and clerics in the Christian faith, both Protestant and Catholic."

Loud groans followed Reed's quotation of Nobel Prize–winning author and Holocaust survivor Elie Wiesel, whose name he pronounced "Elly Weasel."

But Reed's transitions, by and large, were masterful, even elegant. "I believe that anti-Semitism is still a deep and abiding problem in America," he said, hanging his head. "I believe sadly that there is much anti-Semitism today, that is not emerging from the right as it once did, but it is emerging on the left."

Still, the fact that his two examples of leftist bigotry—the Reverend Jesse Jackson calling New York City "Hymietown" while running for president and Louis Farrakhan referring to Judaism as a "gutter religion"—happened to concern prominent African-Americans, not members of the white majority Reed represents, was an inconsistency not lost on the listeners.

————◄○►————

Ralph Reed has in the past been described as having "choir-boy" looks and a "baby face," but neither description does him due justice. At six feet tall and 140 pounds, with rakishly cropped dark hair pomaded into a razor-straight part, Reed might best be described as a suave combination of the young Johnny Carson and James Bond (the narrow-lapeled Sean Connery incarnation, of course).

Reed had arrived late but relaxed for the Whippany event. The plan had been for him to attend a dinner beforehand at the home of Paul Rosenberg, the chairman of the lecture series, held for attendees who had made an additional contribution. "Oh man, do you think they're really bummed?" Reed asked his reception party back at the hotel. By using a back entrance, he avoided direct confrontation with the protesters.

In college, Ralph Reed would "organize the troops" every time a prominent liberal speaker visited the campus. In preparation, Reed would concoct the most difficult question he could to ask the guest ahead of time and then muster up the courage to ask it. Inevitably, the visitor would knock his question out of the park with an impressively polished rebuttal. Public lecturers, he realized, get asked the same questions over and over again. Lesson one: Always have an answer.

After Reed spoke for 45 minutes, a line of 15 audience members formed behind a microphone set in front of the stage for rebuttals. Each questioner had two minutes to ask a question.

"Shalom, welcome. Rabbi Jody Cohen from the Inter-Religion Affairs Department of the American Jewish Committee," said a small-ish woman in a nubby blue-checked suit and white turtleneck at the front of the line.

The rabbi came bearing quotes. Robertson told a Christian Coalition crowd in 1992 that "the first strategy and in many ways the most important strategy for evangelicals is secrecy." And an article published in the *Los Angeles Times* on April 8, 1992, in reference to 1990 school-board elections in San Diego in which Coalition-endorsed candidates won 60 out of 90 local races, attributed the following to Reed: "That's just good strategy: It's like guerrilla warfare. If you reveal your location, all it does is allow your opponent to improve his artillery bearings. It's better to move quietly, with stealth, under cover of night. . . ."

How could Reed, she wanted to know, square these blatant inconsistencies with his just-described philosophy of total disclosure?

Without missing a beat, Reed responded. Religious conservatives, he explained, had been elected in school board elections in San Diego that fall by campaigning primarily in local churches and avoiding public forums and the press. "I was being asked by the reporter whether or not I thought that was a wise strategy," Reed said, pausing to drink from a glass of water. "And I made the mistake of using a military metaphor in describing the fact that it was smart politics to do basic blocking and tackling in grassroots organizing. I now prefer to use sports metaphors, because sports metaphors tend not to scare people. The sports metaphor I would use is this: If you are the New York Giants and you're going to play the Washington Redskins, are you going to photocopy your playbook the night before the big game so that Norv Turner knows all the plays you're going to run? You do not."

Reed had apparently misunderstood the question, but the "misunderstanding" was a timeworn one, a calculated deflective response Reed had used at least once before, when challenged about comments made at a Christian Coalition meeting in Montana comparing the group's tactics to methods of war used by Israelites.

As nettlesome as many of Reed's responses were, I couldn't help but fault the audience in part for its lack of preparedness.

By focusing on well-worn polemical charges such as the Christian Coalition's stealth strategy and Pat Robertson's alleged anti-Semitism (most convincingly traced by journalist Michael Lind in the pages of *The New York Review of Books*), the audience played right into Reed's hands. These were tales of the Christian Coalition in cruder times, before Reed had honed a forthright public persona for the organization.

In response to the accusation that the use of the term "international bankers" in *The New World Order* is thinly veiled anti-Semitism, Reed unfolded a copy of a 600-word response to the charge from Pat Robertson that had been published in the *New York Times.* "I don't know why, but I sort of anticipated this question," he said, with a schoolboy's smirk.

For all of the Christian Coalition's clamorous indictments of the liberal mainstream media, the organization has in recent years turned its dismay into a strategic obsession.

"The natural instinct of newspapers and TV," James Fallows wrote recently in *The Atlantic,* "is to present every public issue as if its 'real' meaning were political in the meanest and narrowest sense of that term—the attempt by parties and candidates to gain an advantage over the rivals."

If what Fallows says is true, the innovation of Christian Coalition operatives like Reed is having learned to exploit that bias to their advantage. If attacked as radicals, they shout that they are the victims of antireligious bigotry, rather than debate the substance of the accusations.

The San Diego school board elections of 1990 proved a turning point in more ways than one for the Christian Coalition. When Coalition-friendly candidates won 66 out of 88 targeted races, the organization was able to gauge for the first time just how powerful its grassroots organizational techniques could be.

But when the press and public subsequently pilloried the group for its "stealth" maneuvers, the Christian Coalition learned how important it was to grow up as well as to expand. Furthermore, many of the school-board winners in San Diego were not reelected. Future Christian Coalition forays into the public sphere were far more polished and defiant.

As Sidney Blumenthal phrased it in the *New Yorker* in 1994, "For the religious right, invisibility is no longer possible." That same year, after prominent Democrats began publicly lambasting religious conservatives for weighting the Republican party unnaturally to the right, all forty-four Republican senators delivered a letter to President Clinton commanding that he renounce the "orchestrated attack on religious conservatives" as "bigotry."

Reed wrote a defining article for the movement for the Heritage Foundation's *Policy Review* in the summer of 1993, called "Casting a Wider Net," which urged religious conservatives to expand their issue base beyond defining issues like abortion and homosexuality. Issues like crime, taxes, and health care, he argued, were also important to the pro-family movement. A rare public glimpse of the dynamic between Ralph Reed and his boss was also bared that year when Robertson disagreed with Reed's backing of the North American Free Trade Agreement during a TV interview. The incident suggested that Robertson, not Reed, still set the Coalition's agenda.

But by January 1995, Reed was confident enough in the Coalition's newly conspicuous position to declare in an address at the Detroit Economic Club that religious conservatives deserved credit for the nationwide Republican sweep in the November 1994 election.

Reed said the Christian Coalition had plans to launch its biggest lobbying effort ever and planned to spend more than $1 million to mobilize "phone banks, fax networks, satellite television, computerized bulletin boards, talk radio and direct mail."

Over 60 million pieces of literature would be published by the Christian Coalition over the next two years, Reed said, "informing people of faith" how closely their lawmakers had adhered to Newt Gingrich's Contract With America.

————◊————

But tonight, from his raised perch, Reed took on all comers. Those audience members with questions had two minutes to ask them; Reed had as much time as he wanted to respond. No time was allotted for rebuttals.

Why didn't you mention Pat Robertson's "fanatical" positions on school prayer, abortion, and homosexuality? asked one emotional young man in a checked shirt and olive khakis who wore a tiny stud in his left ear.

Reed reminded his audience in responding that his organization's position on prayer in the classroom lined up pretty closely with President Clinton's. That his organization's "pro-life" platform covered the rights of the elderly (the Christian Coalition opposes legalizing physician-assisted suicides, for example) as well as those of the unborn.

"Also, you've got some of your facts wrong," said Reed. The Christian Coalition believes, said Reed, that minority protection should be granted based on "gender, age, religious belief, physical handicap, and color," not sexual preference.

And so it went: From the assembled line, twelve people had their questions answered. Most were casually dressed and came off as either intimidated, angry, or ill-prepared.

Only one—Rabbi Marc Disick, director of the Union of American Hebrew Congregations, New Jersey–West Hudson Valley Council—made any headway.

"The core of our religious belief is the belief, from a religious and spiritual place, that a woman has a right to choose an abortion," asked Disick, nattily dressed in a gray pinstripe suit and blue vest. "It's unfortunate, difficult—nonetheless, our religious right. Where can we find common ground in our conversation given my religious premise and your religious premise?"

"I think the reality is—and I cannot speak to your religious tradition, all I know is that I've had orthodox Jewish rabbis explain to me from their religious belief why they were pro-life," Reed responded. "I'm not questioning your theology and—"

"—And I'm not questioning yours," Disick interrupted.

The right-to-life position is not theological to us, Reed continued. It's a "civil rights" position, he explained.

"I think if we could have a little bit of—there is a charge that is made against our community that we care about the child as long as it's in the womb, but then once it's out—"

"I'm beyond that," Disick said. "I'm beyond that."

Reed looked ruffled but stood his ground and began again: "If we could find those who are pro-choice that would just explain *any* abortion that they're against—I mean, there's got to be *some* abortion. I mean, surely if you do a sonogram in the ninth month and you find out it's a girl baby, and you say, We would prefer to have a male, and you kill the child who at that point would clearly survive outside the womb, there's got to be someone who says that's wrong."

Suddenly someone shushed the crowd. Somehow, during Reed's most impassioned and impromptu locution of the evening, the room had broken out in loud conversation. A row in front of me, two men exchanged whispers and laughs and then stood up and left. Reed's incandescent presentation is his strongest suit; when the performance is interrupted, its magic loses its potency.

"I don't know how we begin the dialogue," Reed said in conclusion, "but I don't expect you to retreat from your position, because it's based on deeply moral beliefs. I certainly would hope that you would understand that mine is also based on deeply held moral beliefs."

Disick retorted, "I would accept your counter-case if you would accept my counter-case that if in the ninth month we find out that the life of the baby is threatening the life of the mother, the life of the mother takes precedence."

Now a smattering of applause erupted. A flushed Reed sputtered, "Well, I agree with you there," but his voice was drowned out in the commotion.

"Then maybe we have something to talk about," said Disick.

———◦———

One day in April 1985, the *Washington Post* reported that a group of fifty anticommunist students had constructed a mock prison camp on the west lawn of the Capitol while inside Congress was debating whether to aid Nicaraguan rebels.

The clever bit of street theater, sponsored by Students for America, consisted of students dressed in military fatigues playing guards dragging other students playing prisoners to a makeshift camp site, where they play-acted being beaten and killed. Republican representatives William W. Cobey Jr. and Dan Burton both stopped by briefly to rally the students.

The event's organizer was a recent graduate of the University of Georgia named Ralph Reed. Reed had founded Students for America as an offshoot of the College Republicans in 1984. Financed in part by North Carolina Republican Jesse Helms, the group aided Senator Helms's reelection effort from its headquarters in Raleigh.

Only five months earlier, Reed, as executive director of the College Republicans, told another *Post* reporter of a foiled attempt to send several conservative student groups to the Republican National Convention: "To tell the truth, I wanted to do a pro-Reagan rally but couldn't, because it would violate the tax-exempt status of the groups. I thought something like a God Bless America rally would be a proper vehicle. It would advocate support for President Reagan, but wouldn't talk about his reelection at all."

Reed had turned political animal even earlier. In junior high school, fueled by political biographies, he ran for president of his class under the motto "Vote for Ralph Reed—The Little Giant." The reference was both to Reed's slight build and to Stephen A. Douglas's appellation during his 1858 Senate campaign against Abraham Lincoln.

Reed was born in Portsmouth, Virginia, the son of a Navy doctor and a mother who headed the Methodist Youth Fellowship program at the local church. When the *Atlanta Journal-Constitution* later asked his mother Marcy what her son yearned to be, she responded, "In charge."

In 1981, Reed got his first taste of Washington as an intern in the office of the newly elected Senator Mack Mattingly (R-Ga.), a computer salesman and former state Republican chairman. The Reaganite Mattingly trounced his well-financed opponent (a 67-year-old Democrat whose battles with alcohol abuse and accusations of campaign-fund improprieties received much press coverage) in part by spending the majority of his $600,000 campaign budget on television commercials aired the week before the election.

According to *Politically Incorrect*, the footnote-laden 1994 book by Reed that now serves as a call to arms and a virtual how-to manual for the Christian Coalition, Ralph Reed first met Pat Robertson by accident. The two men were placed next to each other at dinner during George Bush's January 1989 inaugural in Washington.

The 27-year-old Reed was at the time completing his dissertation for a doctorate in American history at Emory, in preparation for a teaching career. (Reed aficionados always use the "Dr." honorific, though Reed himself dropped it on the cover of his book, along with the "Jr.")

Robertson, deeply dispirited, according to some who know him, by his failed stab at the Republican presidential nomination was in search of a repository for the giant mailing lists he had collected during his campaign.

As Reed recalled it in his book, Robertson told him of a plan he had to start a grassroots political organization to further the cause of evangelicals and Roman Catholics.

After dinner, Robertson offered Reed a staff position and recommended that the young grad student draft a proposal for the organization. In his memo, dated February 2, 1989, Reed estimated that American evangelicals numbered "from a low of 10 million to a high of 40 million." By September 1989, Reed was hired as the Christian Coalition's executive director.

Hints at the Christian Coalition's distinguished future, specifically its vanguard double-tiered (some would say Janus-faced) approach appeared from the outset. Although Reed had characterized the startup in his proposal as a "national political organization" geared toward evangelicals and Roman Catholics, he insisted that there be "no spiritual litmus test for membership." This profile is continually run up against the Christian Coalition's official status as a tax-exempt social organization.

Not surprisingly, Reed initially requested a name change for the Christian Coalition, no doubt hoping for one which would provoke less criticism. Robertson refused. (This was not necessarily unwise, considering that Dr. Martin Luther King fostered mountainous change through a civil-rights organization known as the Southern Christian Leadership Conference.)

The Christian Coalition sent its first fund-raising letter to 134,325 supporters of Robertson's presidential campaign. By November 1989, the Coalition claimed 2,000 members and a budget of $82,000.

Today, the Christian Coalition boasts 1.7 million members and 1,700 chapters spanning fifty states. Portraying itself as the McDonald's of conservative activist groups, the Christian Coalition claims it opens one new chapter every day.

"I'm predicting that any day now they're going to announce they have 2 million members," a skeptical Skipp Porteous told me. "Last year they announced they had a million members."

And in fact, some data suggest otherwise: According to the figures that the Christian Coalition must file with the U.S. Postal Service, the net press run for the September 1995 issue of the *Christian American*, the Christian Coalition's bimonthly magazine, was 353,937; for September 1994, that figure was 415,000; September 1993, 275,000; and September/October 1992, 175,000. The *Christian American* is ostensibly sent for free to all dues-paying members of the Christian Coalition. The decrease in circulation between 1994 and 1995 implies that the group's numbers are significantly smaller than it claims and have perhaps declined in recent years.

————<o>————

R. Bruce Skewes used to teach high school English in the New Jersey public school system. He's retired now. According to Bruce Skewes, his politics were once 180 degrees opposite what they are today. As a young man, he was very critical of corporations, the kind of guy who expected the government to solve all his problems.

A jovial, heavyset man in black slacks and a powder blue V-neck sweater, Skewes settled into a chair next to me he had saved earlier with his tweed hat at the Whippany event. "Are you a reporter?" he asked me, having noticed my notepad and tape recorder. Within minutes, he was chatting eagerly and unguardedly about his affiliations.

Two years ago, Bruce Skewes joined the Christian Coalition. Until then, he said, he had never before worked with a political or Christian organization. Today he edits *The New Jersey Reporter,* the New Jersey State supplement to the *Christian American,* the Christian Coalition's national magazine.

Unlike Pat Robertson, Skewes is not a charismatic. "I don't speak in tongues, I don't believe in the word of knowledge," he explained.

We exchanged numbers and business cards and agreed to talk again. A week later on the phone from his home office, Skewes seemed even more at ease as he told me how he first got involved.

Bruce Skewes was raised in a mainline Christian tradition, but in 1976 accepted Jesus Christ as his personal savior. "At that point I began attending evangelical churches," he said. "And one of the things that I noticed was that there were a lot of people in the conservative evangelical churches who felt that political involvement was in some way tainted. That the way to effect change was simply through the gospel and changing men's minds and hearts—and then that would affect the political sphere."

Based on his knowledge of history, Bruce Skewes didn't agree. "I do believe that the gospel is the most important thing that the church does," he continued, "but I also think that one of the things that we're charged with, and by church I mean believers, is restraining the evil in this world."

Skewes's politics were pretty conservative, as one might expect. He was resolutely pro-life ("I respect life and working out that respect by protecting the most vulnerable amongst us, the unborn, from harm—I think that's a principle that pleases God"). He said he believed that multiculturalism and political correctness have cleaved public schools from their primary educational goals, something he said he witnessed in his own English department ("There were not a lot of slaves who wrote great literature during the Puritan period").

During our brief talk, Skewes told me that the National Organization for Women had been "taken over by lesbian radicals" and blamed the media for drastically distorting the views of mainstream Americans in the public square.

"I think it says a lot when you think of the fact that Ted Turner married Jane Fonda," he said. "That really speaks volumes."

None of these opinions really surprised me. If anything, I was disappointed at their predictability. Still, I would have been puzzled had Skewes expressed himself otherwise.

His rhetoric sounded overheated at times, his biases painfully conspicuous. But nothing he said broke the ideological mold. After all anti-Clinton, pro-God, anti-media, and pro-life positions have become the bread and butter of today's conservative wing of the Republican party.

And yet this chance meeting (I just happened to sit in the chair next to the one where Skewes left his hat and coat) convinced me more fully that it was the Christian Coalition's organizational and tactical techniques, not its message, that had triumphed this night.

"People don't separate, the way they properly should, some of Dr. Reed's views," Skewes warned me, "and those expressed on *The 700 Club*." Not that Skewes has any objection to Pat Robertson and the views he expresses on television.

Although Bruce Skewes is familiar with and admires the work of other conservative groups such as the American Family Association, the Family Research Council, and Concerned Women for America, it was the Christian Coalition that spurred him into action.

"I felt that it was important to work from the grass roots up," Skewes said, "which seems to me was the Christian Coalition's philosophy. As a student of history, I was well aware that the Democratic party and socialist progressive people had used this sort of mechanism, somewhat on a cruder scale, going as far back as people like Boss

Tweed and Democratic party organizers, Tammany Hall, even up to the fella in Chicago, Mayor Daly."

Suddenly, in the patient tones of Bruce Skewes's voice, I again heard the voice of the schoolteacher he once was.

I thanked him for his time and asked him how I might procure a subscription to the *Christian American.* He recommended that I call the Christian Coalition's 800 number and ask for the number for the Christian Coalition chapter in my state, rather than joining the national organization. That way, he explained, I would get the *New York Reporter* stapled into my copy as well as many other unspecified extras.

———◁◦▷———

When I called the New York chapter of the Christian Coalition, located in upstate Clarence, the state executive director Jeff Baran, much to my surprise, answered the phone himself. He agreed to mail me some information. He asked for no information other than my name, address, and phone number. Seeming neither paranoid or mistrusting, Baran never questioned my intentions and thus I decided not to reveal them.

For an annual fee of 60 dollars I joined the New York State affiliate of the Christian Coalition (the contribution—although tax-exempt—is not tax-deductible, as all the literature warns). A letter from Baran enclosed with the application urged those who had joined the national office to also join the state office, as well.

It was only a matter of weeks before I got a call from an elderly man letting me know that a Christian Coalition meeting was being held nearby. The New York City chapter would be gathering at the Manhattan Pregnancy Center on East 23rd Street from seven P.M. till nine to discuss church-liaison training and watch a "program from the satellite TV." At least he *sounded* elderly.

The unexpected and secretive nature of the invitation made fantasizing irresistible, although I knew my initial thoughts were far-fetched.

First, I pictured a cabal of middle-aged, urban Klansmen, business types who slipped on their white sheets and hoods over their pinstripes only after securing themselves behind the locked doors of a dilapidated warehouse. Or maybe I would find a bunch of paunchy rogues in overalls with crewcuts and expired union cards assembled in a seedy, wood-paneled room lighted by only a bare bulb. I even half-hoped I would receive a last-minute call with a secret knock or code word in order to gain entrance to the night's event.

I feared only slightly that I wouldn't pass, that upon arriving I would be fiercely interrogated until my true, un–Christian Coalition-like sentiments were laid bare.

Of course, I already knew that the Christian Coalition had a reputation for attracting the best and the brightest minds of the religious right. So at the very least, I expected Hobbesian technoweenies in rep ties and tassel loafers.

———◦———

On a slushy Tuesday evening in January, I headed for the Manhattan Pregnancy Center, which as it turned out, was located in a small run-down building, five floors up from a storefront. As I stepped out of the tiny elevator I was directed down the hallway by a tall smiling man wearing a red Santa Claus hat, apparently on his way out.

The Manhattan Pregnancy Center turned out to be a tastefully appointed doctor's suite with navy-print Ikea sofas, a grandfather clock, and a well-stocked magazine rack.

It was no surprise to discover only four other attendees, not including myself. After all, this was Manhattan, traditional enemy territory for conservatives.

What I discovered, however, exceeded even my wildest expectations: I was the only man.

A friendly woman I'll call Connie introduced me around and then turned toward me and asked how I found out about the meeting? Her Gucci loafers, charcoal tailored wool pants, dark tan, and silk scarf draped loosely over her shoulders all bespoke New York savvy.

I tried to act calm as I wracked my head for a suitably matter-of-fact response. "I got a phone call," I said. And that was that.

For the next hour, we sat under a framed pen-and-ink drawing of a mother and child (the mother looked like Mrs. Cleaver) plotting our course.

Connie was the group's leader. A petite, energetic woman in her mid-thirties, Connie looked and acted like a Madison Avenue public-relations executive.

Then there was Sadie, pudgy and disheveled, who looked to be in her late fifties. With her denim skirt and tangled gray hair, she could easily have been mistaken for an aging earth mother. But Sadie informed the group her favorite 1996 presidential candidate was Alan Keyes, the most unabashedly religious of the Republicans, whose platform was wholly composed of moral issues.

Chauncey was the real-life embodiment of Martha Stewart. A tall, matronly Upper East Sider who used to live in a Westchester suburb, Chauncey spoke in oval tones as refined and silvery as her hair.

Connie began the meeting informally by advising everyone to help themselves to the mounds of literature she had laid out on the low, wide coffee table. Sample voter guides, photocopied newspaper clips, and pamphlets labeled Contract with the New York Family (a localized corollary of the Contract with the American Family) cluttered the coffee table.

Connie offered a stapled packet to each of us on the night's topic, the role of the church liaisons in the Christian Coalition. Also available for the most enterprising among us, comprehensive, spiral-bound Citizen Action seminar guides, from which the church-liaison handout had been photocopied.

"There's also an audio tape here somewhere," Connie said, looking toward me, the newcomer, "but it's basically just someone reading the same guide word for word."

Repetition turned out to be the watchword of the evening—a central Christian Coalition precept, it turns out. Connie proceeded to flip open her notebook and read from her copious hand-written directives, which were essentially a recap of what was in the photocopied packet.

Approach the pastor or elders of your church. Tell them about the Christian Coalition ("give them one of these," she said, passing around handfuls of a glossy flyer called "From the Pew to the Precinct"). Ask them if you can distribute nonpartisan church guides and run a voter registration drive at the church. If you are met with resistance, suggest forming a "civics concern ministry," which would distribute voter guides and run registration drives.

Connie added her own bits of New York–related political information—"Remember the presidential primary is March 7. . . . Don't forget the New York City school board elections are in May!"—but the rest was straight out of the book.

"Which candidates is the Christian Coalition supporting?" asked Bunny, a svelte young Asian-American woman with long, feathered-back hair wearing a bright fuchsia business suit.

"The Christian Coalition doesn't endorse candidates," said Connie, calmly but firmly, as she scanned a chart of Manhattan voting preferences by district that she had pasted to the cardboard backing of her notebook.

Connie had determined that only 15 percent of Manhattan voters voted consistently conservative and therefore standard Christian Coalition neighborhood-coordinator strategies, such as randomly knocking on doors, "are pretty much going to be a waste of time."

She was repeating the math and wisdom of a formula the Christian Coalition has previously referred to as the "15 percent solution." Sixty percent of the Americans qualified to vote are registered; 30 percent of those voters determine the outcome of the presidential election; of those 30 percent, 15 percent determine the outcome. As Guy Rodgers, national field director for the Christian Coalition, put it in the eighties, "We don't have to worry about convincing a majority of Americans to agree with us. Most of them are at home watching *Falcon Crest.*"

This was why, Connie said, the church-liaison program was so crucial in New York. "Does everyone have a church they think they might approach?"

———◦———

The Christian right movement first stumbled upon the template for the church-liaison strategy in the mid-1980s.

In the 1970s, religious leaders and conservative movement operatives realized their common ground, particularly in the wake of a 1978 IRS ruling against the tax-exempt status for Christian academies.

"Back then, most fundamentalists weren't even registered to vote," said Skipp Porteous, cofounder of the Institute for First Amendment Studies, a religious-right watchdog group. Porteous, a former fundamentalist preacher who later renounced his conservative-Christian affiliations and began publishing *The Freedom Writer,* a left-leaning newsletter subtitled "A Hard Look at the Hard Right," recalled the time he first witnessed religious conservatives nosing their way into the political arena.

"I started getting involved in what we now call the religious right in '75 through a church in California called the Church on the Way," Porteous said. The renowned conservative church in Van Nuys recruited Disney actor Dean Jones and singer Pat Boone to lead a series of "God and Country" voter-registration rallies in state capitals. Porteous headed up the New York State rally in Albany.

"Strangely, I wasn't that conservative in my politics," added Porteous, pointing out that today's hot-button topics like abortion were rarely played out in black-and-white political terms by fundamentalist Christians of that era.

"It wasn't until 1977 when conservatives like Paul Weyrich and Richard Viguerie got together and realized that if you could make conservative Christians think that abortion was murder," Porteous said, "it would be a tremendous way to get people involved in politics."

By the early eighties, those same conservatives had begun recruiting like-minded Christians, most prominently through the group known as the Moral Majority. For many in the mainstream, the Reverend Jerry Falwell, de facto leader of the Moral Majority, soon epitomized all that was right-wing and Christian in America.

By matching church membership lists to voter records, conservative operatives ably targeted unregistered church voters and began registering them. The results of the registration drive were successful enough to win both Falwell and Robertson a space on the podium at the 1984 Republican National Convention.

Chauncey said she had already tried approaching the pastor at Redeemer Presbyterian Church on Madison Avenue, where she happened to be a member. "And they expressed no interest," she said. "I have no idea why—Redeemer has already declared itself a pro-life church."

Sadie, too, had inquired at her house of prayer in Greenwich Village, to no avail. "Our pastor is weird," she said, munching a handful of pretzels she had grabbed out of her tote bag. Later she whispered, "He's very liberal."

"Can you think of a specific church you might approach? Where do you belong?" Connie asked me directly.

I told her that I was in the process of moving, which was true, and that I had initially been attracted to the Christian Coalition through political angle and hadn't given the religious angle much thought yet (also true).

If only there were a better way to ferret out people who "thought like us," Connie lamented.

Near the end of the hour, a late guest arrived, a stout, beady-eyed woman in a long wool overcoat and full makeup. Susan, in her mid-thirties, was not a member of the Christian Coalition but a leader from a local, sympathetic pro-life group.

She was a member of Redeemer, too, and added that she would feel uncomfortable approaching church leaders at churches she didn't belong to.

"Isn't there any other way to find out who these voters are, if they're male or female?" asked Bunny, the relative newcomer of the group. "Then I would know where to look for them."

Connie had already compiled a list of 400 conservative voters in Manhattan, but she hoped to expand that list. If they could get at least a thousand names together, they could make best use of the "phone tree" they were hoping to purchase soon.

The New York affiliate's purchase of their very own phone tree was a hotly anticipated prospect. Once the chapter was in possession of a phone tree, a newfangled dialing device, they would be able to prerecord a short message and then automatically dial 999 phone numbers and play the message for whomever answered.

Susan said she might be able to get a local database from her group.

"You know, we all really have to put a whole lot more work into this," she continued. "You have to realize that groups like the GMHC [Gay Men's Health Crisis] don't just have a couple activists sitting in a room once in a while. They have hundreds of activists working all day, every day, convincing people to donate loads of money for AIDS research. That's why there's more money being spent on AIDS research than on cancer research, even though not nearly as many people have AIDS. I've got nothing against AIDS research, but I get a letter from the GMHC every single year even though I've never sent them a dollar. I still can't figure out how they ever got my address in the first place."

"It's probably because you subscribe to *New York* magazine or something," offered Connie.

"Hey, I subscribe to *New York!*" Bunny chimed in.

"Did anybody see this article in *The New York Times?*" Connie, clearly pleased with herself for having changed the topic to something more upbeat. Seconds later, we were all holding photocopies of the news piece.

It told of a proposal introduced in Colorado by John Patrick Michael Murphy, a personal-injury lawyer and radio talk-show host, to eliminate property-tax exemptions for most churches and nonprofit organizations as a cost-cutting measure. Someone had scrawled "Is New York the next stop for this effort?" in the margin.

Everyone quickly admitted this seemed unlikely considering the fact that, according to the *Times* story, widespread concern over the growing influx of evangelical Christian organizations into Colorado was the main drive behind support for the initiative in that state, a scenario incredibly unlikely to duplicate itself in New York.

"Who is the Christian Coalition supporting for president?" Bunny asked. The Christian Coalition does not endorse candidates, Connie stated as calmly and evenly as before.

Bunny thought she had read before in *The New York Times* that the Christian Coalition "favored" certain candidates.

At this point, Susan launched into a tirade about how biased and liberal the *New York Times* was. But Bunny came to the *Times*'s defense, arguing that their detailed coverage of church affairs was the best in New York. "But I *love* the way the *New York Post* has been attacking Hillary Clinton," she added. "Has anybody here been reading the *New York Post* lately?"

Nobody else had been. "I sometimes steal the bike messenger's copy," sniffed Connie. "I really should look at it more. It's really fun."

"It's really *conservative*," said Bunny, with wicked grin.

Everyone also agreed that *The Wall Street Journal* was a good read although not technically a New York newspaper. And that the title of a new book by *Saturday Night Live* writer Al Franken—*Rush Limbaugh Is a Big Fat Idiot*—was pretty funny. But then Susan, who said she worked for the publisher that was releasing the book, started complaining about how relentlessly liberal book publishers were, except Christian book publishers.

Suddenly, Connie flopped her notebook closed and let out a big sigh. "New York is pathetic!" she said, with all the outrage of the peppiest cheerleader on the losing team's squad.

I piped in that New York ought to be looked at as a monster challenge rather than a lost cause. A quote from Ralph Reed popular among supporters reads, "To succeed in politics it is more important to light a candle than to curse the darkness." But Connie's frustration was understandable.

Having run out of material in her notes, she again urged everyone to help themselves to as many brochures as they wanted. "But I'm going to need two dollars if you take one of those," she warned, as I reached for a spiral-bound seminar guide. After I forked over the cash, she admitted, "I was sort of surprised myself when I ordered these and they showed up with a bill."

Tonight's meeting was supposed to culminate with a closed-circuit TV broadcast—*Christian Coalition Live!*—received via a roof-top satellite dish that was hooked up to a 25-inch color monitor in front of us. Unfortunately, it was only eight o'clock and the hour-long program wasn't due to start till nine.

Chauncey, Bunny, and Susan all said they couldn't stay. "I wonder why they don't just make videotapes of it?" said Bunny. "Then we could have our meetings whenever we wanted."

"Someone should run downstairs and buy a blank videotape," Susan said, having noticed the VCR on the shelf beside the TV.

Connie told us that anybody with a satellite dish could watch the program, except for the second half hour. "Really?" asked an amazed Susan. "Why?"

Part two was a strategy session for Christian Coalition members only. That's not the kind of information you want everyone to get ahold of, Connie said.

On that note, the three women put on their coats and left.

Being alone with Connie and Sadie for an hour was of concern only because I feared that if the talk turned to God and the Bible, I might accidentally reveal my lack of conviction. My fear proved unfounded; neither God nor Jesus Christ nor the Bible ever came up. Certain beliefs were presumed. The conversation instead focused on politics.

Why, I thought to myself, does a religious organization concern itself so much with politics and so little with religion?

I only had to look at another one of my handouts for an answer ("Christian Coalition's 5-Fold Mission" read the heading). Goal number one was to "represent the Christian point of view before local councils, state legislatures, and Congress." Number two involved publicly proclaiming the group's values. Three was to train leaders for taking action, both social and political. Four, to inform Christians on these issues. And five, "to protest anti-Christian bigotry."

All of these aims presume that there is in fact a unified Christian point of view, a dubious claim even within the movement. The first and third are forthright enough but would seem to call into question the Christian Coalition's classification as a tax-exempt "social welfare organization." (Section 501(c)(4) of the IRS code requires that the Coalition's focus remain primarily nonpartisan.)

Under the ever-increasing scrutiny of its opponents, the Christian Coalition has in recent years expertly fine-tuned its game plan to test the borders of the IRS classification.

When a person's religious faith informs each life decision, as is presumably the case for nearly every member of the Christian Coalition, no doubt separation of church and state is tricky business.

In *Politically Incorrect*, Ralph Reed writes of what he calls a "common misunderstanding" about the First Amendment. He acknowledges that the Constitution explicitly forbade the government from establishing an official state religion. "But equally important," Reed observes, "the 'free exercise' clause of the First Amendment prevented the government from restricting the citizenry from worshipping God according to the dictates of their conscience of freely expressing religious ideas." What's the point of religious liberty, Reed argues, if it's permissible only in church on Sunday.

It's no wonder Christian Coalition members repeat their organization's mission like a mantra. Understanding morality not informed by a faith in Jesus Christ must confound true believers at least as much as values not guided primarily by common sense perplex the rest of the population.

At ten minutes to nine, Connie unlocked the coat closet to the left of the television, dug a loafer into the upholstered seat of one of the waiting-room chairs, and began fiddling with the decoding box perched on a high shelf.

After Connie informed us that Representative Bob Dornan of California—one of the Republican candidates for president—was scheduled as a guest, Sadie lit up.

Dornan was Sadie's second choice for president, after Alan Keyes. Sadie once found herself alone in an elevator with Bob Dornan at a Republican fund-raiser.

"You'd look great with a ponytail," she'd told the balding conservative. Sadie explained that she just loved men with ponytails.

"Actually, my son has one and it doesn't look half bad!" he responded.

Slowly, Connie conjured up a static-filled picture. *Christian Coalition Live!* is broadcast live on NET, the fledgling public-affairs channel founded by conservative pundit Paul Weyrich.

"Help yourself to some cashews," said Connie, ripping open a plastic bag of nuts and tossing it on the table.

Hosted by Ralph Reed, *Christian Coalition Live!* turned out to be a public-affairs–style program with two armchairs and a minimal stage set.

The ruddy-faced Dornan had the hoarse voice and brusque manner of a raunchy standup comedian. So even when the subject was serious—such as Bosnia, where, he told Reed, he visited just a few weeks earlier—Dornan's eyebrows raised up and his mouth formed a horizontal crescent moon.

Things are much worse in Bosnia than the mainstream media is letting on, Dornan reported. Clinton is in over his head.

That's pretty impressive information, said Reed.

You're hearing it straight, Dornan said. That's why I went over there, he said. The soldiers Dornan spoke to couldn't even explain why they were over there, he said. One soldier took him aside and said, It's all about politics, isn't it? Why, Clinton wouldn't even let our boys go home for Christmas, he said.

"Remember, Clinton doesn't even have the constitutional right to send troops to Bosnia," Dornan added, at the end of one gruff rant.

Like regular commercial TV, the program was divided into segments and interrupted by commercials (oldies CDs from Time-Life, *Golf Digest,* the complete Stephen King, and Sally Struthers shilling for that dopey correspondence school). And like the tabloid talk-show hosts recently reviled by conservatives (Dornan himself has a radio show), it was light on real information, heavy on sensational rhetoric, and occasionally entertaining.

Reed ended the half hour by proudly reporting that the Christian Coalition currently had 300 satellite downlink sites across the country, but that they were hoping to have 1,000 in place by election day.

I actually came out of the first half hour feeling a little bit better about Bob Dornan. If he dropped out early (a likely prospect that begins sounding likelier when Dornan starts listing everything he likes about his "good friend" Bob Dole), he could always start a career as a blowhard comedic personality of the Rush Limbaugh variety. Upbeat and fast-talking, Dornan would make a good infomercial personality, the kind that might sell you a knife set you knew was crummy just because you knew it would make him smile. And compared to the follow-up act, he was downright hilarious.

(Bob Dornan later blamed the Christian Coalition for his last-place finish in the Iowa caucuses. The Christian Coalition inexplicably omitted Dornan from their ubiquitous voter guides. "Without having the money to be able to campaign in Iowa, without having the time because of work here in Congress, there was one voter guide that was circulated that was important for us. And we weren't in it," Theresa Cobban, Dornan's daughter and campaign manager, told the *Los Angeles Times.* "For whatever little campaign we had, we had the rug pulled out from under us." Dornan finished in tenth place with only 131 votes, well behind "No preference," which received 297 more.)

At the next commercial break, Connie was up on the chair again, making additional adjustments for the second members-only "strategic" half-hour.

The show soon returned, to the very same setting, except there was a new guest, Brian Lopina, billed as director of government affairs for the Christian Coalition. A thick-necked, white-haired man with pleasant, youngish features violated only by a densely creased forehead, Lopina was substantially less magnetic than Dornan.

Reed asked Lopina whether he thought that infighting among the Republican presidential candidates would lessen the chances of a Republican taking the race. Yes, said Lopina, in-party sniping makes that party's candidate lose. Then Reed rattled off examples of past presidential candidates from both parties who lost after protracted primary battles.

Lopina then recommended that the "troops" call their elected representatives and register their opinion on the $500-per-child tax credit that "the Democrats want to rescind." A list of names began scrolling across the screen, "key leadership targets," Reed called them. The list began with prominent Republicans like Newt Gingrich, Dick Armey, and Bob Dole and dwindled down to lesser known Republican names. Lopina said it was up to the "troops" again.

More lists followed. The next pinpointed elected representatives who "needed encouragement to continue supporting a balanced budget and tax cuts." This list was more far-reaching and was arranged by affiliation, with the most conservative first and the "Blue Dogs," the coalition of 21 Democrats who proposed a middle-of-the-road budget-balancing solution, at the end.

In the middle were the moderate Republicans—"Republicans who sometimes get nervous when they are attacked by the media," Reed cracked.

Then Reed took a few viewer phone calls. One caller from Alabama wanted to know who the Christian Coalition would suggest supporting for president. "Let me know if you have any suggestions," said Reed, talking through a wide, nervous laugh. The Christian Coalition, he explained, was not a partisan organization and therefore would not be supporting any specific candidate.

"But I will say this," Reed continued. "Bill Clinton is the first presidential candidate to run unopposed in a primary since Harry Truman." (Reed somehow neglected to recall Ronald Reagan's bronco-busting unilateral run in '84.)

After another commercial break, Lopina was replaced by Camille Mitzner, a business-like young woman introduced as a grassroots liaison for the Christian Coalition. Mitzner told Reed that calls to Congress were terrific but they weren't enough. Send letters to the editor of your local newspaper when you read an anti-Christian article. Call in to local radio programs and voice your opinion.

"Be sure to be polite and stay cool," Mitzner suggested. "Try not to yell."

Reed took some more phone calls. A viewer from Alabama wanted to get some more information on "phone trees." These are wonderful devices, Reed said. He explained that they were available in models that range from $300 to $1000. The most expensive hooks up to a computer. Phone trees, Reed explained, could be purchased through the Christian Coalition.

Another caller asked for an elucidation of the anti-Christian comments made by a national radio personality. The reference was to National Public Radio (NPR) commentator and author Andrei Codrescu, who, during the December 19, 1995, edition of NPR's *All Things Considered*, had said—referring to Christian conservatives— "The evaporation of four million [people] who believe this crap would instantly leave the world a better place."

Without mentioning Codrescu's name, Reed called the utterance an act of anti-Christian bigotry. He reported that he had demanded an on-air apology from NPR, which had been granted. This was not enough, though, he said. National Public Radio must be privatized.

Reed also took this time to mention another bout with anti-Christian bigotry, perpetuated by *GQ*, "a liberal magazine." An article in the January 1996 issue of the men's fashion periodical by Scott Raab had mocked the Promise Keepers, a Christian men's movement founded by former University of Colorado football coach Bill McCartney.

Reed did not refer to Raab by name. He simply said that the article "referred to Bill McCartney as Adolf Hitler." (Although Raab never actually wrote this, the piece did compare one of McCartney's football-stadium oratorios to a scene out of Leni Riefenstahl's pro-Hitler documentary *Triumph of the Will*. Later, Raab tries the line on a reporter from the German magazine *Der Spiegel* who likes the line and asks Raab if he can use it.)

Finally, the meeting had come to an end. As Connie, Sadie, and I put on our coats, Connie asked me what I thought so far. I told her I thought it was "neat," figuring *neat* was a good fifties term.

"Where do you go to church again?" she asked. I've been moving around a lot, I said. Then came the zinger I had feared: "What denomination are you?"

I paused for a moment and then told my one lie of the night. "I was raised Lutheran," I said (not true). I picked Lutheran, figuring that too unusual a response would arouse suspicion but that Lutheran was exotic enough a sect that chances were she'd have no clue what to say next.

My instincts proved correct, and as the three of us headed out I thought to myself that these women seemed to be pleasant enough people, people who cared.

In the lobby, Connie pushed on the first of the double doors to the street but it stuck. I looked through the window and saw that a middle-aged woman, covered in a ragged wool blanket, was sleeping in the vestibule and blocking the door.

We knocked on the window and the woman started to get up, politely apologizing as she gathered her things.

Connie searched her purse for a pass she said she had for a free meal at the Church on the Bowery. But she couldn't find it. When the homeless woman opened the door, we all carefully slipped by and all apologized for disturbing her.

"Watch out for your shoes," said Sadie as she tried to close the outer door. Connie was already on the sidewalk straightening her fur coat.

Within seconds, we were all walking down the street, in conversation again.

———◄○►———

Back in September of 1995, the Christian Coalition jumped into the 1996 presidential race with a big splash by luring all of the major

Republican candidates (except Arlen Specter, a vocal Coalition opponent) to its annual Road to Victory conference in Washington.

A consummate inside-the-Beltway operator, Ralph Reed stocked
his pool with big Washington fish. The speakers' roster at Road to Victory '95 was chock-full of appearances by conservative heavyweights
like Newt Gingrich, Dan Quayle, Bill Bennett, Phyllis Schlafly, Tom
DeLay, Kay Coles James, John Kasich, and Robert Casey.

"I read in this morning's papers about how all these candidates
were coming down here to court all of you," Senator Bob Dole, back
then the probable Republican front-runner, told an audience of 4,000
on September 8. "Well, maybe we are. What's wrong with that?"

Although Senator Dole had received the Christian Coalition's
ultimate seal of approval, 100 percent accordance on their congressional scorecard, for the three previous years, he had stopped short of
signing a pledge sponsored by a Phyllis Schlafly–sponsored group
called the Republican National Coalition for Life to fuse a staunch
pro-life position to the Republican platform. As a result, jeers of "Sign
the pledge, sign the pledge" accompanied his entrance.

"Don't look at pledges; look at the record," Dole grumbled. He
later assured the audience, "You're going to have a big, big say about
what happens in '96."

Senator Phil Gramm, the first major candidate to drop out of the
race in February, took a far more sanguine position toward the Christian Coalition than Dole at the Road to Victory gathering.

"I signed the pledge," Gramm boasted to a cheering crowd earlier
the same day. Gramm also praised school prayer, tax cuts, and the death
penalty while vowing that, as president, he would never command U.S.
troops to serve as part of United Nations international forces.

"There's only one person who's ever lived who I would trust to
impose values on America," Gramm added. "And when He comes
back, He won't need government to impose his values."

Lamar Alexander suggested in his speech that it could hardly hurt
the nation if the next president "were not a little bit of a preacher."

"We need to do more than win an election or win the House or
win the presidency, my friends," Pat Buchanan bellowed. "We need to
make this beloved country of ours God's country once again."

Pat Buchanan, who was introduced by Oliver North and joined on the podium by Pat Robertson and Ralph Reed, was by far the most obsequious of the candidates.

Having been handed the conference's most coveted spot, Buchanan seemed poised as the Christian Coalition favorite (no endorsements!).

Buchanan's fiery public presence coupled with his calls to do away with familiar demons of the Christian right like the Department of Education, affirmative action, international trade agreements like NAFTA and GATT, and those "miserable secular humanists in sandals and beads" made him a natural Christian Coalition ally.

But Ralph Reed and Pat Robertson are political pragmatists. They wanted to win.

And statements made by Buchanan, a former television commentator on CNN's *Crossfire*, at Road to Victory '95 implied that he might not weather the mainstream.

"Together, my friends, in the words of Micah, let us go forth from this place to do justly, to love mercy, and to walk humbly with God," Buchanan intoned, "for the time is not far distant when we're all going to have to gird ourselves and take that long march up to Armageddon to do battle for the Lord."

Buchanan even referenced Pat Robertson's "new world order" conspiracy theory (a gesture that must have chagrined the propitiatory Reed), pointing to the World Bank's recent loan guarantee to the Vietnamese government as evidence.

In the months ahead, however, Bob Dole emerged as the Republican Party's best hope for beating Bill Clinton: a moderate conservative with strong name recognition and maximum appeal.

Wary of getting marginalized, Ralph Reed and the Christian Coalition continued courting all the Republican candidates. Conservative columnist Robert Novak wrote that Reed had Dole's ear and had brokered a deal with the candidate to lay off pressing the Coalition's most controversial demands.

By February, it appeared the Christian Coalition and its founder, Pat Robertson, had gotten their utmost wish: Pat Buchanan, a genuine pro-life, God-fearing social conservative, won the New Hampshire primary without compromising his firm stance.

But while Buchanan's narrow lead confirmed the Christian Coalition's power to galvanize conservative religious voters, it also raised the question of whether the Christian Coalition actually got what it wanted or really needed.

At Road to Victory '95, Buchanan was handed the coveted keynote speaker slot at the event's gala banquet.

The Friday before the New Hampshire primary, at the Christian Coalition's preprimary God and Country Rally in Manchester, New Hampshire, Buchanan returned the favor by trading his defining message, a protectionist U.S. economic policy, for one that vowed to combat abortion, government intrusion, gun control, and higher taxes.

But Ralph Reed expressed concern to the *Washington Post* about any candidate spouting overly fervent America First rhetoric, explaining that "a lot of conservative evangelicals are involved in small business, especially in the South, and these are often primarily export driven."

And Pat Robertson, the chairman of a multinational public corporation, International Family Entertainment, could appreciate the value of international trade more than most. IFE has for-profit business interests in Asia, the Middle East, and Africa. (One recent rumor had Robertson negotiating with the Chinese army to service mainland China with original TV programming.)

"I will never walk away from you," Buchanan promised the gathered Christian Coalition members in Manchester, adding he would be "the most pro-life president ever."

In the days after the New Hampshire primary, prominent Republicans like General Colin L. Powell and Governor Christine Todd Whitman lined up to disavow Buchanan as an extremist incapable of appealing to the party's less rabid voters, Reed and Robertson no doubt knitted their brows.

In 1988, Pat Robertson ran for the Republican presidential nomination and placed a strong second in the notoriously conservative Iowa caucuses, behind Dole, but then faltered.

Reed had spent the last few years trying to broaden the Christian Coalition's agenda and constituency, ever since the 1992 Republican National Convention, where Pat Buchanan's divisive speech purportedly alienated moderate "economic" Republicans.

Furthermore, the Christian Coalition, now the most organized (and loudest) activist group in the nation, had proven its influence. In 1988, conservative Christians had only Robertson. In 1996, they had no fewer than four viable Republican candidates jockeying for their cause.

Theirs was a tough choice. While Buchanan more closely represented the Christian Coalition's socially conservative agenda, his ability to take the presidency remained in question. "He has very strong support in the Christian Coalition but he by no means has unanimous support," hedged John Dowless, head of the Christian Coalition in Florida, in February, hunkering down for his state's March 12 primary. Dowless predicted (or was it hoped?) Dole would take Florida, where he said Buchanan had "no organization" and where Dole's campaign had been "very effective in recruiting religious conservatives" ever since the previous November when their candidate placed first in the state's Presidency Three poll.

Regardless, the Christian Coalition was forced to take a similar approach with each upcoming primary skirmish: Acknowledge the substantial support for Buchanan while gently shepherding toward Dole.

Could it be that the Christian Coalition got more than it asked for? If so, it is conceivable that the organization's finely tuned tactics now worked only too well. Pat Robertson and Ralph Reed had finally met their match: a candidate too far to their right for their purposes.

By drawing conservative religious voters to the candidates who most accurately and honestly represent their social agenda, the Christian Coalition runs a constant risk of being isolated, and thus rendered ineffective, by its own potency within the Republican Party.

CHAPTER TEN

---◆---

10:00 A.M., April 29, 1994

W ell, ladies and gentlemen, we've got something that's a little explosion today," says Pat Robertson. "Her name is Paula Jones." Only moments before, Robertson was consoling a perky Terry Meeuwsen about her seven-year-old's horrible mosquito bites, which she had dutifully tended to the night before. We're mere seconds into today's broadcast of *The 700 Club*. Once the shiny gold *700 Club* logo on a royal blue background is whisked away to strains of canned game-show–style theme music, the camera pans across a bank of television monitors, one of which ripples with the familiar soothing image of Robertson. Then the word "Newswatch" joins the *700 Club* logo in gold at the bottom of the screen. While the high-tech map of the world floats in the background, the set looks more like that of a daytime talk show, with freestanding armchairs rather than a news show's desk and image prompter. Then the camera swiftly hones in on the set and its occupants. From left to right sit Ben Kinchlow, Terry Meeuwsen, and Pat Robertson. Kinchlow and Meeuwsen face Robertson. Broad, genuine-seeming smiles all around. A cube-shaped table is lodged between them with coffee mugs for Meeuwsen and Robertson. (Robertson himself eschews both coffee and alcohol.) "Well, thank you and welcome, ladies and gentlemen, to this edition of *The 700 Club*. We're delighted to have you with us," says Robertson. The words "Pat Robertson" hover below Robertson's face. Today he is resplendent—sky-blue shirt, white collar, dark navy suit, and a red and black brocaded tie as thick as a rope. His silvery-red hair is combed so nicely in front that it looks like cotton candy. Robertson's legs are crossed; his hands are clasped but relaxed as he turns toward Meeuwsen and says, "We understand you had a difficult night with your little ones." As he speaks Robertson unhitches his hands and thrusts them toward Meeuwsen, fingers open, as if he might hug her. The tone is light. The level of patter is something akin to that of Regis and Kathie Lee on their ABC morning show. The camera zooms in on Terry Meeuwsen, brightly dressed in a stylish orange-and-crimson-striped ensemble. It's the mosquitoes, she explains, and the fact that it was 3:15 in the morning when she returned from the Dove Awards in Nashville. Robertson swivels back to the camera. As breezily as he chatted about mosquitoes ("They say pollen is up 20 percent in this area") and the Dove Awards, he broaches the topic of Paula Jones. He explains that Jones, a former employee of the Arkansas state government, has a "shocking" story that she has revealed to CBN News in an exclusive interview. It's a teaser for a story to be aired later in the broadcast. Something about a 1991 incident with the then-governor of Arkansas, but Robertson gives no name. A short video clip of Paula Jones sitting on a leather couch follows immediately. Jones looks to be a young woman in her mid-twenties. Her face, framed in a full headshot, fills the screen. She is dressed up in a cornflower-blue print dress, full makeup, and bright-red lipstick with formal gold earrings. The fifteen-second snippet features Jones describing how someone, clearly a man, exposed himself to her in his office. A quick shot of a bearded male sitting next to her on the sofa, presumably Jones's husband, is intercut with her brief testimony. The look on his face is one of rankled concern. Back to Robertson, who gently intones, "This is something you might not want your children to watch when we get into the piece—but she's a hit, on today's Newswatch." Judging from the rest of the highlights, this day's *700 Club* is a typically eclectic mosaic. Some other features: a piece on residents of Cape Henry, Virginia, and their crusade to have their community officially and legitimately declared the first landing site of America's English settlers. Another will celebrate the thirtieth anniversary of the CBN Phone Counseling Center. News footage ostensibly comparing social progress in South Africa and bloodshed in Rwanda segues into a discussion between Robertson and Kinchlow, who is black, of how the white American civil-rights types who were always up in arms about apartheid in South Africa overlook the killing in Rwanda because it is primarily black-on-black violence. An update on the American Center for Law and Justice's success in challenging rulings against protest restrictions ("bubble zones") at abortion clinics and prayer at university commencement exercises is followed by a brisk tête-à-tête between ACLJ's chief counsel Jay Sekulow and Pat. Soon enough, there's another teaser for the Jones interview. Robertson recommends viewers to stay tuned for the interview with the former Arkansas state employee. "It's shocking," he says as a placid image of Jones strolling along a beach with her husband and infant child glides across the screen. Now for a commercial, or rather a public-service–style spot for *The 700 Club* "Newswatch." Generic footage of soldiers with guns in camouflage gear, a man getting wheeled into an ambulance on a stretcher, a house on fire, a house ravaged by a hurricane, and a train crumpled up like an old tin can. Natural disasters are God's way of expressing his displeasure, an interspliced image of Pat Robertson explains. Ben Kinchlow in another disembodied video blurb alludes to riots that are only going to get worse as people move away from God. Although what Kinchlow is referring to is not evident from his words, a shot of chanting marchers in a parade (one sign clearly reads "Lesbian Rights") makes things a little clearer. As an unidentified Hispanic man testifies that *The 700 Club* news broadcasts live up to a higher standard, a shot of Kinchlow, Meeuwsen, and Robertson on the job is faded in. Back to the disaster reel as a phone number, the number to call in order to join *The 700 Club* pops up in the lower margin of the screen. Contribute and you'll bring "life-changing news" to millions. Like public television, this advertisement says, *The 700 Club* needs the help of viewers to provide a viewpoint unavailable elsewhere (clips of Kinchlow, Meeuwsen, and Robertson, each standing outside with a microphone and presumably reporting from a remote location). Finally, it's Paula Jones time. Not surprisingly, the female Terry Meeuwsen, not Robertson, introduces the story. As she introduces the segment, the corners of her mouth slouch into a kind of happy frown, the very expression a young mother might make to comfort her child about an unpredictable circumstance that, as unfortunate as it might be, cannot be helped. Like mosquitoes, for instance. Jones, Meeuwsen explains, alleges that the former governor of Arkansas made sexual advances toward her. "Her name is Paula Corbin Jones," Meeuwsen says. "He is Bill Clinton, the president of the United States." Before the cut to the interview, Meeuwsen gently counsels the audience as to the feature's graphic content, "offensive to all of us, but especially for your children." A quick jump to a clip of Clinton walking into an unspecified official engagement, then the same one of Paula Jones on the beach with the man now identified as her husband Steve, to whom she was engaged at the time of the alleged incident, and their son. Back to the footage of Paula Jones ("the daughter of a Nazarene minister") and Steve on the leather couch that led off the broadcast. A voice-over (male announcer, no discernible southern accent) explains that Paula Jones spoke to CBN not only about the circumstances surrounding Bill Clinton's alleged advances but also about how the American press had ignored her story. CBN's Dale Hurd, a doughy thirtysomething man with a moonish face and mustache, sits across from Paula Jones. The camera lens rests on him while he describes the scenario as it allegedly took place in May 1991 at the Excelsior Hotel in Little Rock during a state-sponsored event. Hurd says Danny Ferguson, an Arkansas state trooper, approached Jones at the reception desk where she was working and informed her that the governor wanted to meet her in his hotel room. What did she think was going to happen? Paula Jones then appears on-screen, seated on the tan leather couch, admitting that she was initially excited about the opportunity to meet the governor. She had never met him before and she asked her friend Pam if she thought it would be okay to go to the governor's hotel room and her friend Pam said that she thought it would be fine and maybe he would even offer her a job. The word "excited" comes out "ex-*aiah*-ted"; when she recounts her conversation with her friend Pam, she says Pam told her "Who's knows, Paula, he *maight* offer you a job." The door to the hotel room was already cracked, Jones says, when she arrived. "He shook my hand and introduced hisself." The conversation began with a little small talk about her job and about her boss. Jones alleges that Bill Clinton told her he "lahkd ma curves," and then tried to "kiss on me, and kiss on my neck." Paula Jones continues talking but the image switches to Steve Jones, her husband, who is taking a big breath and purses his lips. Of course, Paula had told the governor she had to leave, she says. But before she did, he stood up, and exposed "hisself," and dropped his pants. Paula Jones's next utterance is about as raunchy as any you're ever likely to see on the Family Channel. She tells her interviewer that the governor asked her to "kiss it." She pauses, swallows, and widens her eyes like a little girl who just found out her father was a mass murderer. Or rather, she looks *up* at the camera. The camera, you see, is fixed slightly above her line of vision. And Ms. Jones wants to make one thing perfectly clear: When Bill Clinton asked, she refused. Paula Jones has already filed an affidavit under penalty of perjury, says an unseen announcer, as an enlarged copy of the affidavit fills the screen (the words "penalty of perjury" are at the exact center). Unlike when Anita Hill, who is shown, filed suit against Supreme Court justice Clarence Thomas, also shown, Paula Jones has corroborating witnesses, the male voice says. Pamela Blackard ("Pam") has also filed a sworn affidavit. Now that affidavit fills the screen. Another voice, this time female with a southern accent, presumably Pamela Blackard's, is heard reading the text of her affidavit which is typed in large, bold white letters in a box set on a background of blazing orange and blue. The content of Pamela Blackard's affidavit, as read and printed on the screen, is relatively disappointing. It states merely that, according to Blackard, Arkansas state trooper Danny Ferguson did invite Jones to Bill Clinton's hotel room on May 8, 1991, at approximately 2:30 P.M., and that, upon returning fifteen to twenty minutes later, "expressed a full range of emotional distress in recounting her encounter with the Governor." Another corroborating witness, Debra Ballentine, states in her affidavit (printed, but clearly not spoken by Ballentine, since the voice is that of the same woman with the southern twang that read Blackard's testimony, and who therefore is, evidently, not Blackard either) that on January 4, 1994, Ferguson joined Jones and Ballentine at their table at the Golden Corral Steakhouse in North Little Rock, Arkansas, and affirmed that he had arranged the meeting between Jones and Clinton. Although the down-home female voice says "Ferguson joined Ms. Jones and I," the words on the screen read "Ferguson and I(SIC)," thus acknowledging a common grammatical mistake for text-bound viewers while never betraying the authentic emotional quality for those viewers whose understanding of the issue is deepened simply by the sound of a woman, apparently distressed, with a comforting accent. Suddenly, the male announcer butts in. "Trooper Danny Ferguson could not be reached for comment," he says. But what we're looking at for the split second that it takes for those words to be spoken is a calm river with a cityscape behind it. Perhaps it's li'l ole Little Rock. Fortunately, articles in the conservative *American Spectator* (cover and magazine spread are shown) and *Washington Times* (the newspaper's front page, with a photo of Clinton and headline that reads, inexplicably, "Clinton denies profit, cuts loss on Whitewater") featuring interviews with Arkansas state trooper L. D. Brown allegedly confirm Jones's "description of a womanizing Bill Clinton." But in 1991, state employee Paula Jones had no reason to expect what would come to pass. We watch a sweeping shot of the majestically modern Excelsior Hotel as a lead-in to an irksomely familiar round of questioning back on the leather couch. "What did you expect, going to the room?" asks the obsequious Dale Hurd. "*I was excited, who wouldn't be?*" says Jones. A squishy, forlorn sense of dread overcomes me as Jones reappears on my screen. Her tightened, frightened voice rises and cracks as she answers the same question again. Perhaps she is a victim, I wonder. What chance does a young, helpless woman have against a man of power and position? Husband Steve tells Hurd that Paula is a little bit "naïve." He says he means "trusting" but he uses the word "naïve." The male announcer explains that the only reason Jones pursued her claim was to fend off accusations that she had willingly participated in another sexual encounter with Clinton. At this precise moment, we are watching Steve and Paula Jones reading *Choo Choo, Peek-a-Boo* to their infant son. She first went to *The Washington Post* with her story, but at the time of this broadcast they had yet to print it. A *Post* reporter working on the story was even suspended, the announcer intones, as we scan a close-up of a headline and byline of an article, actually an article from the same *Washington Times* issue shown before. The headline reads "Post sex story gets the spike" and there is no indication as to why the reporter might have been suspended. Hurd then asks Steve Jones—not Paula—what he thinks of Bill Clinton now. Steve says he reckons the guy's got some pretty deep psychological problems. All Paula Jones wants to do is make right what was done wrong to her, she explains. Lots of rumors have circulated about "him," Jones says, since she has gone public with her accusations. She never again repeats his name. And so we return to the studio. Pat Robertson is aglimmer. "I know if you feel like I do, you feel like the breath's been taken out of you," he says, most sensibly, as the camera returns to the studio. These are allegations, Robertson reminds, just allegations, but the rumors are mounting and it's hard to imagine that the truth will be obscured forever. *The President is like a father figure. Our presidents are so important to us.* You be the judge, he seems to say. Don't we expect better from our most prominent of public officials? It is reasonable to wonder why the seamy allegations continue to gather. "As a cool medium TV has, some feel, introduced a kind of rigor mortis into the body politic," wrote Marshall McLuhan. "It is the extraordinary degree of audience participation in the TV medium that explains its failure to tackle hot issues." But where is the failure here? Robertson's producers have slalomed down the slippery slope that is this touchy topic with grace and verisimilitude. Oh, TV craft of this brisk surety must in itself reward its makers. Imagine the speeded-up rush as the deft editor whirred his reels, instantly and expertly orchestrating the brief Jones interview, her languid descriptors oddly concupiscent, alongside the atmospheric mood and landscape footage and the announcer's promptings with their defiantly independent logic. This must be what it is like for the expert ski racer, rounding each marker so close that the flag brushes one's cheek yet knowing each near-miss is a tribute to the jagged-out, gravitational groove. Proven facts are hard, and difficult to press through the bit-mapped tube. But the fibrous, loamy innuendos of this rich, mythic tale are perfect matter for Pat. The whole frothy shebang lasts a crisp ten minutes, brazenly brief by traditional text standards, but action-packed and deeply felt on contemporary TV's terms. (Ever notice how the first forty minutes of *Late Night With David Letterman* are a hyped-up lead-in to the last twenty, during which each of the three guests have three to five minutes to penetrate your living room?) Emotion, not details, is the news Paula Jones is delivering. You'd have gotten that, regardless of where in those ten minutes you tuned in.

————◦————

By the sheer force of its proliferation, *The 700 Club* has occasionally scooped the mainstream media, albeit usually at the behest of news-makers, like Paula Jones, who happen to have a partiality toward CBN. In June 1985 25-year-old Laura Walker Snyder revealed to Pat Robertson on *The 700 Club* how she and her mother decided to turn in her father, accused Soviet spy John Anthony Walker Jr., to the Fed-eral Bureau of Investigation. Following a 1982 religious conversion, Snyder had called in to CBN's counseling center for guidance in set-ting right a shattered family situation in which her estranged husband had taken away their son. Based on the anonymous advice she received, she urged her mother to turn in her father. Federal indict-ments later revealed that John Walker led an espionage ring that included Snyder's husband and younger brother. Her son on her lap, Snyder told Robertson on the air, "The Lord heard my cries and saw my tears. He told me He would return my child to me." When Ten-nessee policeman Gary Dockery emerged from a seven-year coma in February 1996 the story received much national publicity. But his par-ents gave exclusive interviews to *The 700 Club,* where they reported that it was their faith in God that had brought their son back to con-sciousness.

CHAPTER ELEVEN

On the Web

C^{lick}. . . . When I enter "Pat Robertson" as my query in Alta Vista—a powerful and impressively accurate Internet search engine made by Digital Equipment, which I run through my Netscape Navigator—and activate the Submit button with my computer cursor-pointer, it spits back a list of what the program estimates to be "about 40,000" hits, or possible matching entries.

The first thing I notice is that no matter how technologically adroit he might be, out here on the gloriously infinite Infobahn, Pat Robertson can hardly muster up a respectable level of control: The first 50 entries I pull up are mostly reprinted magazine articles attacking (and mocking) Robertson for his attacks on—among other targets—homosexuals, e-cash, and computer bar codes.

One is simply the random observations of a student at the University of Illinois who happened to stumble upon "Pat Robertson and gang" on *The 700 Club:* "Ok . . . Have you watched this show? This IS funny *sheeit*. My friend made me watch it tonight and we were on the floor. First of all, we think the object of the show is to try and make the other two laugh. They do this thing called 'Word of Knowledge.' Anyways, they go around the panel and each person gets informed by God who his healing power will reach. [At one point] Robertson says 'I'm feeling an indentation in your forehead and God is straightening your skull.' My friend told me that he gets really pissed at the show and calls the number but the operator won't let him on the show because he says stuff like this: 'Hi, I just prayed with Pat and I think he's full of SHIT!!' "

Entry No. 55 is the first that appears to be Robertson-sanctioned. So I again click my mouse—this time, my pointer is on the Internet address listed as "http://www.cbn.org/cbn/people/pat.html."

With that, I am whisked away to a copy of Pat Robertson's impressive curriculum vitae, complete with full-color photograph and brief history of Christian Broadcasting Network. It hails Robertson as the founder of Regent University and Operation Blessing, but makes no mention of the Christian Coalition or the American Center for Law and Justice.

The last paragraph even provides a bracingly succinct answer to a question that has long confounded many: "In 1961 Robertson was ordained a Southern Baptist minister in Norfolk, Virginia. He resigned his ordination in 1987, prior to announcing his candidacy for the U.S. presidency. Therefore, Robertson should no longer be identified as 'reverend.' "

Click. . . . I've depressed the Home icon at the bottom of the page and now find myself at *The 700 Club*'s home page (in World Wide Web lingo, that's "http://www.cbn.org/index.html").

"A Light Shining in the Darkness" reads a banner across the top of the screen. A hulking royal blue *700 Club* logo, in superhero-style 3D lettering, takes up most of the space on an ominous black background. On the Web, where cool graphics and high-definition sci-fi vibes get a site bonus points, CBN has gotten off to a pretty good start.

From here I can choose any of nine "links," or connections, to other related sites.

If I click on *The 700 Club* link, I'm introduced to cohosts Ben Kinchlow and Terry Meeuwsen, and Pat Robertson, host of *The 700 Club*. There's a *Good Morning America*–style color promo photograph and a text description on a pleasant corporate-gray background with other links embedded in it.

At the Ben Kinchlow link, I learn that he was ordained in the African Methodist Episcopal Church, that he has written three books, that he was in the Air Force, and that he has three children and six grandchildren. No mention here of his early-life drug problems or his years spent as a Muslim prior to his born-again transformation.

Terry Meeuwsen's link reminds me that Meeuwsen got her start as a singer with the New Christy Minstrels, that her duties as Miss America 1973 lasted only a year, and that although she became an official *700 Club* cohost in June 1993, she "has been a familiar face on *The 700 Club* since the early 1980s."

When I click on the words "275 U.S. television stations," I'm jettisoned to a list of 46 state links (plus the District of Columbia), behind each of which is a list of "free" TV stations where *The 700 Club* can be found in every state.

I learn here that, were I not a cable subscriber, I could watch *The 700 Club* on WLIG, Channel 55, in New York, from noon to 1:00 P.M. every weekday. I also discover that CBN apparently doesn't have affiliates in New Hampshire, Massachusetts, Rhode Island, or Wyoming (they're not on the list). And that in Pennsylvania, *The 700 Club* is rebroadcast on so many stations, I could pretty much watch the same show over and over again from dawn till dusk.

Back at *The 700 Club* link I can access highlights of the upcoming month's shows; read about the new Sunday version of *The 700 Club;* I can even fill out a pledge form in order to join the club (you must donate between $20 and $83 to become an official member; for a contribution of $417 or above, you can join the highest echelon, the Founders Club). Interestingly enough, under the list of titles to choose from on the blank pledge form, the appellation "Ms." is included along with "Miss" and "Mr. and Mrs." Is it possible that the technological revolution taught social conservatives something the feminist movement couldn't?

Through a *700 Club* link titled "Ministry" I find another called "Teaching," which is described as "on-line tracts and literature." I select one link called "The Christian Perspective on Halloween," which informs me that the original Halloween was no children's holiday but a day for the ancient Celts and Druids in Britain and Ireland to consort with the devil. The paper concludes that well-meaning Christian parents might tape religious pamphlets to each piece of candy they distribute to trick-or-treaters as an antidote to the holiday they otherwise wish would disappear.

Under the "Newswatch Today" icon are transcripts of key news stories from the past two months' programs. For February 1996, most are diatribes accusing the Clinton administration of covering up the Whitewater affair and White House adviser Vince Foster's death.

———◄○►———

Pat Robertson's virtual presence on the Internet in some ways is an apt metaphor for the real-world Pat Robertson. If the Internet hadn't developed organically, no doubt someone like Pat Robertson would have invented it.

The World Wide Web, essentially an amalgam of computers around the globe randomly linked by common technology, was tailor-made for sophisticated, multilevel communicators like Robertson. Hypertext, the Internet term for the hidden pages of text that are linked to a home page through embedded path connectors, is a Robertson dream. Your mouse pointer takes you only as far into the information tree as your curiosity guides you. If you remain interested, you never know what you might find. And each further click on an embedded phrase or link brings you deeper into the new mindset.

It's easy to understand why the more traditional media, such as newspapers and network television, had long confounded narrowcasters like Robertson. Until recently, the crown of media legitimacy most frequently went to whoever had the funds and wherewithal to create a sense of that legitimacy. Yes, knowledge, expertise, reliability, and establishment credentials have always played a role in the development of preeminent media outlets. But appearances count for an awful lot as well.

Pat Robertson has spent his career seemingly testing each level of legitimacy—examining what it looks like, what it feels like, and how much money it costs to become a world-class player in that sphere—and then setting about to duplicate that legitimacy on his own secular terms.

In corners of the public square where traditions ran deep or the startup costs were prohibitive (founding a university; or building a fourth television network, as Robertson was planning to do in the mid-1970s), the results were always spotty.

Creating what is essentially a mirror "bizarro world" equivalent to mainstream life as most Americans know it must be, by any measure, a Sisyphean endeavor.

But on the Internet, that familiar stratification of legitimacy doesn't exist. Large multinational media conglomerates like Time

Warner and News Corp. have already lost millions of dollars trying to distinguish themselves on-line. Pimply college students can now log on to powerful university mainframes and construct elaborate "home pages," decked out with embedded sound files (.WAVs) and real-time videos (.MPGs or .MOVs) as fascinating as—if not more fascinating than—any produced professionally.

As portrayed in the mainstream "liberal" media, the Robertson empire is an unwieldy octopus, multiple for-profit and nonprofit arms attached to a big, fat megalomaniacal head. But on the Web, Robertson has it his way: As he has frequently claimed, many of his organizations are distinct and independent entities. In Internet-World, that is the virtual truth.

———— ❮○❯ ————

Only when I slip out the Internet's equivalent of the back door, *The 700 Club*'s "text-only" contents link, do I discover a list of other Robertson Web sites, under the heading "Friends and Neighbors."

Here I find the first mention of other Robertson affiliates. I click on the "Christian Coalition" link (http://www.cc.org/) and launch myself into a whole new aesthetic environment.

Where *The 700 Club*'s Web pages are muted and reassuring, the Christian Coalition's are brash and vibrant. I am greeted by a giant red, white, and blue Christian Coalition banner and the group's stylish half-moon logo.

I click on the link called "Welcome" and am introduced to Pat Robertson, president, and Ralph Reed, executive director (color photos for both and welcoming messages—you can actually hear Reed read his if you download the audio file).

Of all of Pat Robertson's homes on the Internet, the Christian Coalition site is the most information-packed. I access a database of enhanced versions of the coalition's infamous congressional scorecard, with a link for each state, which lists that state's representatives in Congress and how they voted on issues important to the Christian Coalition. A big blue check mark denotes a representative having "voted or announced" in favor of the Christian Coalition position; a big black X connotes the opposite.

An explanation of each issue ghosts the whole database; here I learned that the issue abbreviated as "Taxpayer-Funded Pornography" on the scorecards refers to the amendment introduced to Congress by Jesse Helms in 1993 that would have restricted National Endowment for the Arts grants only to nonprofit organizations, and prohibited individuals from receiving these grants. It was rejected in the Senate, according to the text, 65 votes to 30.

Had I not clicked on the link, I wouldn't have received this fairly significant clarification. Of course, the Christian Coalition didn't technically conceal this information from me—but it didn't exactly share it with me up front, either.

The names of many of the senators and congresspeople are linked directly to their e-mail addresses in Washington, so visitors to the site can fire off a high-tech gripe while the bile is still bubbling.

Another feature archives the full text of the *Christian American* magazine (a valuable tip if you'd like to read it without joining the Christian Coalition).

Through the "Speeches and Position Papers" link I learn that the Contract With the American Family—the Christian Coalition's elaboration on Newt Gingrich's Contract With America—recommends legislation to restrict Internet access to pornography for both children and adults. Not really in the spirit of things, considering how much the Christian Coalition has made of its own free access.

Eager to move on, I backtrack to *The 700 Club* site and browse down the list of choices again. When I try the American Center for Law and Justice site from here, I pull up a golden shield on a black background along with a message that informs me this site will be "coming soon."

A more fascinating find is the Asia Pacific Media Corporation's home page. A quick scan of the wordy materials here reveals that APMC is a business concern, chaired by "Dr." Pat Robertson. Founded with the intent of providing venture capital for Pacific Rim "media projects," the whole site is an invitation and how-to kit, presumably to be found by would-be Asian start-ups. The literature explains that, while APMC has no connection to IFE or the Family Channel, Robertson and his officers gained their expertise running those ventures.

There's no mention of CBN, no mention of Christianity, although the literature does make clear that APMC will only be backing projects that "promote positive moral values."

Regent University's Web site not only explains the school's mission but also includes links to the home pages of Regent students.

———<o>———

It occurs to me that what all these sites have in common is a heightened sense of interactivity. All provide voluminous amounts of information and encourage the net-surfer to respond, either to the sites themselves or to outside (i.e., mainstream) receptors.

By contrast, the Web site for Operation Blessing, Robertson's missionary arm, feels canned. Except for a few color photographs, one shows workers unloading food from trucks, another a doctor caring for a child, and a third is of an L-1011 wide-body jet, slated to become a "sophisticated flying hospital." (Mel White reports that the airplane-hospital—a project that Robertson has had in the hopper for more than a few years—to date has never taken off.)

Most significantly, the Operation Blessing site has no interactive features whatsoever (last time I checked).

Frank Rich of *The New York Times* recently reported from the first "alternative" (read "liberal") Media and Democracy Congress conference in San Francisco. Most so-called progressives, Rich lamented, were so desperately behind the curve when it came to communicating via new media. "Were the alternative media locked in their own insular world, in which only National Public Radio beams in news from the outside?"

Rich's assessment might have been a trifle harsh. To be fair, National Public Radio itself has an impressive, information-filled Web site. And the American Civil Liberties Union has a home page that easily rivals the Christian Coalition's in sheer quantity of information, if not in interactive capabilities.

But Robertson and his conservative technocratic cohorts (familiar names like NET's Paul Weyrich and Family Research Council's Gary Bauer) turn up a lot.

———◄o►———

The only way I was able to find anything more than a mention of the Family Channel on the Internet was by initiating a brand-new Alta Vista search (neither *The 700 Club* nor the Christian Coalition site offered any clues).

As it turns out the Family Channel's presence remains minimal on the Internet, barely a facade of the large network.

CHAPTER TWELVE

The University

E ducation is one of the few topics on which most Americans can agree: They're in favor of it.

Add issues like federal aid, school vouchers, and curricula debates to the heap and education obviously becomes as complicated a subject as any other.

But at its essence, the subject is sacrosanct. Some education is better than none, goes the old saw, and kudos to anyone that can get young people excited about learning.

I suspect that's one reason why Harvey Cox, a liberal Protestant Harvard theologian who published a story in *The Atlantic Monthly* last year recounting his visit to Pat Robertson's Regent University as a guest lecturer, gently rebuffed my requests for an interview.

"What you want to do that for?" he said, I believe jokingly, when I explained that I was trying to sift out Regent's effect on mainstream academia.

Cox's article, "The Warring Visions of the Religious Right," looked within Robertson's university, which had invited him to lecture on his research of the Pentecostal movement worldwide, to find a surprising amount of academic dissent, and thus vibrancy, on campus. His piece concluded that Regent University was a welcome moderating force in light of the dominion-theology movement, a conservative Christian ideology that places Judeo-Christian biblical law above any and all constitutional law.

While Regent University, by Cox's estimation, eschews the so-called premillennial perspective (an end-time scenario favored by many twentieth-century Christian fundamentalists which teaches that civilization will deteriorate and the world will crumble until Jesus Christ returns), it fosters—and sometimes embraces—the postmillennial worldview.

Postmillienialists believe that righteous human beings, essentially servants of Christ, must achieve positions of influence in societies in order to prepare the world for the Messiah's return. While the postmillienialist eschatology appears more positive, its real-life enactment is far more terrifying.

At its most extreme right, postmillenialism includes figures like Rousas John Rushdoony, the leader of the Christian Reconstructionist movement. The prolific Rushdoony, who is based in Calaveras County, California, has published books recommending the death penalty for homosexuals, adulterers, astrologers, witches, and misguided teachers. Christian Reconstructionists believe applying a strict biblical law on modern society to be a prerequisite for the Second Coming of Christ. In his writings, Rushdoony criticizes "the heresy of democracy" and interprets the Old Testament as requiring the death penalty for kidnapping, bestiality, homosexuality, witchcraft, and the "rape of a betrothed virgin."

Even at Regent, which some today call the Harvard of the religious right, the harsh reactionary threat is a real one. In 1993, Robertson fired Herbert Titus, then the dean of Regent's School of Law, for what amounted to institutional insurrection based on Titus's strict dominion views.

When Robertson founded his graduate-level university in 1977, he dubbed it CBN University; in 1990, he renamed it Regent University to better reflect the school's mission. Apparently, some had been confusing it for a broadcasting school.

A *regent*, Robertson told the press at the time, is "one who governs a kingdom in the absence of a sovereign. We are training you to represent the sovereign."

But when the first eight professors arrived in the fall of 1978 to build a graduate university from scratch, representing the sovereign was the least of their worries. To start with, few had any experience teaching above the undergraduate level. "I remember asking the question, 'What do I do differently at the graduate level when I teach television and broadcasting,' " one professor recalled. "And I don't know if we had an answer, except that even in 1978, this studio was better equipped than CBS in New York—everything was brand-new and state-of-the-art."

The first class of 77 students had CBN's broadcast facilities, worth an estimated $22 million, at their fingertips.

Today's Regent University encompasses schools of business, law, government, divinity, counseling, and education. Regent's College of Communication and Arts includes schools of journalism; communication studies; performing arts; and radio, television, and film. Of the over 1,400 students attending Regent, according to the school's own literature, over 48 percent are married; the average student age is 34; and approximately 14 percent are minorities.

The law school, which opened in 1987, has become the university's largest, best-known, and most controversial program. Housed in the recently built Robertson Hall—a grand, contemporary knockoff of Philadelphia's Independence Hall that sits beside Robertson's own oversize on-campus manse—it is also the closest to Robertson's heart.

That said, Regent law school has warred incessantly with the American Bar Association since its inception. In 1986, Oral Roberts University's beleaguered law school, which went to court for provisional ABA accreditation but later failed to win full accreditation, shipped east its law library along with some of its faculty members and students.

Since then, the ABA has taken the School of Law to task for, among other things, its baldly religious agenda and for allegedly lying about its tenure policy.

Confirming the suspicions of Robertson opponents, *U.S. News & World Report* in 1995 ranked Regent's reputation in the bottom fifth percentile for American law schools, awarding it last place in academic reputation and near-last in reputation among judges and lawyers.

But as with so many of Pat Robertson's operations, Regent has carved itself a niche. A year after the *U.S. News & World Report* study came out, Thomas Brennan, a former chief justice of the Michigan Supreme Court, released a study that declared Regent 59th out of 179 American law schools, a ranking that put it ahead of every other law school in Virginia except the University of Virginia.

In February 1996, the university got a much-needed shot in the arm when Kay Coles James, a former U.S. Department of Health and Human Services assistant secretary from the Bush administration, resigned as Virginia's secretary of health and human resources to become dean of Regent's School of Government.

Indeed, Regent, more than any other arm of Robertson's empire, seemed to interface most convincingly with the world around it.

———◁o▷———

Dr. Alan Snyder, an associate professor at Regent's Robertson School of Government, has a career path as uniquely confounding as any at the fledgling university.

Born in Indiana, Snyder attended the in-state Purdue University and later received a doctorate in American history from American University. He first worked for Pat Robertson from 1973 to 1976 as a late-night DJ on the Portsmouth radio station, a job he left to become the headmaster of Berean Christian Academy, a parochial school in the area.

In 1988, while still finishing his dissertation, Snyder got a call from Regent (then CBN U.) to fill in for a professor on sabbatical. Snyder left for Indiana Wesleyan University when a full-time position didn't open up at Regent, but leapt at the opportunity to return five years later, because "I really felt like this was where I was supposed to be."

Although Snyder had taught at secular universities with better reputations than Regent's, such as George Mason University in Fairfax, Virginia, he described his post in Virginia Beach as "the most advantageous teaching position I've ever had, and it's the most fun."

Snyder told me that, unlike elsewhere, he never felt the need to censor himself at Regent. While Snyder was at George Mason in 1984 and 1985, a student lodged a formal complaint against him. "Basically, I was very positive about faith working in American history," he explained, "and I was critiquing the liberal perspective governmentally and it rubbed her the wrong way."

Snyder was not asked back; he became convinced that institutional bias against his particular perspective was the reason. (I'd wager that Dr. Snyder's assessment of the scenario was correct.)

At Regent, Snyder can teach American history in a way that is informed by his faith. He gave as an example: "I know that in my American Founding course I make it very clear to students that when you look at the First Amendment you don't find the words 'separation,' 'church,' or 'state.' What you do find is that people are free to practice their religious belief without interference from the national government. And the national government cannot set up an official church, which is far different. You might want to use the term 'separation of church and state' but it has to be understood properly. It never meant separation of faith from life or from government service. So that's the critique that I bring to it and I think that that's probably the same one Pat Robertson has."

It's this practice of reading history as if it were some immutable map for the future that maddens mainstream academics. While it's true that the phrase "separation of church and state" appears nowhere in the Constitution (it actually emanates from a letter Thomas Jefferson wrote to the Baptist Association of Danbury, Connecticut, in 1802, in which he interpreted the First Amendment), the point is simply one of semantics. To most people such literal interpretations of legalese are mere instances of the cart leading the horse.

To hear a Regent faculty member parroting one of Pat Robertson's greatest hits hardly came as a surprise, but Snyder insisted that Robertson, who is on the university's board of trustees and who holds the title of chancellor, has little hand in the institution's day-to-day affairs.

"It's the same way that Margaret Thatcher is the chancellor of William and Mary," Snyder explained. "She's hardly there."

Somehow this didn't reassure me. So I sought out other members of the Regent community to test Snyder's claim.

Regent University's World Wide Web site proved a useful resource to this end. That's how I'd found Snyder in the first place. Before we talked by phone, we exchanged e-mail. His home page even featured a full-color photo of him (dark hair, heavy-lidded eyes, probably in his mid-forties).

The sheer proliferation of student and faculty home pages posted on Regent University's Internet node alone connotes a level of institutional porousness I had yet to experience while trying to interact with any of Robertson's other organizational arms.

Another Regent professor I met on-line, one who helped found the communications school, boasted of the numerous points on which he and Pat Robertson diverged. He introduced himself during our first phone conversation by saying, "I'm Roman Catholic, you know" and went on at great lengths to convince me of Regent's "every-college" status.

He's a registered Democrat, he told me; and so is Terry Lindvall, Regent's president. "The best lesson of what control does this guy have over any of us," he said, "was to walk to the parking lot when Pat was running for president and to see all the bumper stickers that weren't Pat Robertson's—none of us agreed with his running, but he didn't ask us and we weren't about to tell him."

Religious pluralism, he said, is ultimately what Regent is after. Considering its roots in nondenominational, charismatic Christianity, I figured that this goal seemed at least plausible.

According to Regent's figures, 28.7 percent of its students identify themselves as nondenominational. The most widely represented denomination is Baptist (15.4 percent); followed by Assembly of God (12.5 percent); Presbyterian (5.6 percent); and Pentecostal (3.6 percent). Four percent of the remaining attendees said they were Catholic. A substantial 19.6 percent registered their religious affiliation as "other/unknown."

But unless that 19.6 percent is made up of Moslems, Jews, Mormons, Hindus, and atheists, Regent's dream of academic assimilation seems unlikely. For all its modern-world sheen, the university touts its offerings as a "Christ-centered" graduate education. "Through this diversity of educational offerings," reads one glossy brochure, "Regent has graduated God-fearing men and women who are impacting nearly every sector of society in our nation and around the world." One would presumably already have to be partial to a very Christian viewpoint or a very conservative one to be drawn to such a school.

Stephen Magnuson, who is currently enrolled in a joint-degree program at Regent's law and government schools, fits the former profile. The son of a Baptist pastor, Magnuson grew up in Iowa and Nebraska before spending four years of active duty in the Marine Corps. He was considering law school at University of Nebraska when a roommate in the Marine Corps who happened to be a Regent alumnus turned him on to the school. "I had never heard of Regent until I got this new roommate," he admitted.

The 28-year-old Magnuson was, however, familiar with its founder. "Frankly I was kind of hesitant to come to a school that was run by Pat Robertson," he said. "Being a Baptist pastor's kid, I grew up in a vein of Christianity that was slightly different than Pat Robertson's—more mainline, fundamentalist, conservative. We don't tend to have the big TV programs and the TV preacher kind of things."

But after a look at Regent's curriculum and faculty credentials, Magnuson changed his mind and decided he would take his lumps for graduating from "Pat Robertson's university." He described how he had been "pleasantly surprised" by the way the school's history courses "take you back" to the origins of the United States.

"When you study law and you study government a lot of schools start with the here and now and don't have a real understanding of where we came from," he explained, "and so they don't have a real understanding of where we can go."

One of Magnuson's favorite classes traced American law back to its common-law and scriptural roots and concluded, according to him, "it doesn't matter where you go to practice law, this is at its foundation." Regent advocates learning about where we came from, not "declaring this place a theocracy, saying our goal is to elect a Christian leader and make the Bible our law," according to Magnuson.

But, he admitted, "if you're going to deny that the Bible has any kind of foundational relationship to our theories of government then there's not much you can discuss on that level."

Still, he was adamant: "The bottom line is that pragmatic arguments still fall short—well, maybe a little more money will help or maybe a little more of this will help. In order to get to the bottom of an issue you've got to talk principle, you've got to talk morals."

The soft-spoken Steve Magnuson sounded to me like Regent's version of a liberal. Throughout our conversation he repeatedly reassured me that he didn't think the Bible should supersede constitutional law, only that "Judeo-Christian principles" needed to better inform modern-day legal discourse.

Pat Robertson no doubt would be proud. Legend has it he staked his claim on the empty lot in Virginia Beach after learning that it was not far from Cape Henry, where English settlers arrived in 1607 and raised a large cross before founding Jamestown. As I learned from a CBN tour guide, Robertson has gone so far as to trace his roots back to the pastor that ministered to the original boatload.

Founding a university was Robertson's best shot at legitimately reclaiming that history. An accredited institution of higher learning designed to train Christians to infiltrate society with godly principles would irrefutably yoke Robertson to the United States' pre-Constitutional heritage. The esteemed Harvard College, after all, began in 1636 as a training ground for Puritan ministers. Besides, a successful academic institution would bring along with it an intellectual and organizational heft that a prosperous company or ministry alone could not.

When Robertson first got the idea for CBN University in 1975 he envisioned it as a Christian school for students from Third World nations; later talk turned to establishing an undergraduate college just for juniors and seniors.

"What I wanted," he told one biographer, "was older students who were already pretty much set in their life's pattern and who wanted to get the training needed to focus on a major career goal." Possibly commenting on his own college experience, Robertson added, "I didn't want a bunch of kids who were still trying to have big parties and grope around in life in more than one way."

Steve Magnuson has nothing if not direction in his life. He told me he hoped to effect social change through lawyering, a goal made evident by his current work with the National Legal Foundation, a conservative legal action firm started in 1985 by Robert Skolrood, who formerly headed Robertson's now-defunct Freedom Council Foundation. "My true desire is to move back West somewhere and work on property law," Magnuson said, "and try to get the EPA [Environmental Protection Agency] off the backs of the farmers and ranchers."

But Magnuson, his missionary-like zeal aside, hardly could be counted among Robertson's flock. He readily admitted that he had never watched a full episode of *The 700 Club*, never read any of Pat Robertson's books, and never called in and/or donated money to Robertson's ministry. "I figure I give him five thousand dollars a year for tuition," he quipped, "that ought to be enough."

And when it comes to Robertson's politics, Magnuson remains at more than arm's length. He said he had no taste for the chancellor's conspiracy theories ("you know, the whole 'the world is run by three Jews' kind of thing"), but added that those views held little bearing in the university setting.

Still, Magnuson described his Regent classmates as being on the whole both socially and politically conservative, although he recalled one fellow student having done an internship in the liberal Senator Ted Kennedy's office prior to coming to Regent.

"That's not to say that there aren't people who differ on issues," he added. "Like when we bring up welfare reform as a topic of discussion there are people who think the government should be heavily involved in the support of the poor and there are people who think the government shouldn't be involved at all."

————◇————

"I'm going to be kind of blunt here," said Kevin Danford. "Are you a Christian?"

As I sputtered out my unintelligible answer at the other end of the phone it occurred to me that this was a first. Before now, in the course of researching this book, no one had confronted me with this incalculably rude question. Up until this point I had only read about the legendary born-again brusqueness (Pat Robertson's *Shout It From the Housetops* is brimming with such tales, where brusque is passed off as boldly righteous). I was beginning to think the young, bellicose Christian soldier was a mere figment of the liberal imagination.

Kevin Danford—a 1995 alumnus of Regent's joint program in public policy and business (he got two master's degrees in three years)—presumably the very conservative kind of Regent graduate, proved me wrong.

Danford said the only other graduate program he considered, other than Regent's, was Harvard's. He would have attended Harvard had he been accepted—"I made a small mistake on my application," he explained—but he was convinced Regent had provided comparable if not superior preparation for his future.

"What attracted me was Regent's mission statement," Danford said. "The whole idea that the campus was designed and the programs and everything was designed for this one purpose: To teach excellence in academics but with a Biblical viewpoint. There are many Bible colleges and you can be a dummy and still get in, but I like to be challenged. Regent has a balanced approach—it wasn't about coming in and being indoctrinated, it was, 'Hey, take a look at what we think is a good approach.' "

Having grown up the son of a military chaplain and received his undergraduate degree from Evangel, a small Bible college in Springfield, Missouri, Kevin Danford was pleased to discover that he could continue his education at what remains the only freestanding graduate-school university in the country. He, too, first heard about Regent from a friend who is an alumnus.

After graduation, Danford became a salesman for Herbalife, a weight-loss and health-product vendor that, like Amway and Mary Kay Cosmetics, has been compared to fundamentalist Christianity for the heightened spiritual environment it provides for its employees, who sell person-to-person rather than through stores.

Weekly appearances on *Youngbloods,* a round-table political talk show broadcast on Paul Weyrich's National Empowerment Television network—"I'm the ultraconservative voice," he said—satisfied his political ambitions.

"The strength of Regent," Danford opined, "is the combination of the academic approach which says, Look, you ought to be willing enough to examine various opinions, and the strong belief that Pat Robertson infused into the institution, which is, Let's present a Biblical view and then let's talk about it"—he recalled the 1994 campus visit of Walter Sullivan, a Catholic bishop from Richmond considered controversial due to his belief that homosexuals should be welcomed into the church—"and where we might be wrong, let's do some adjusting."

This kind of talk ought to prick up the ears of opponents to Regent's narrowly channeled educational perspective—not because of its reasoning, but because of its cumulative effect. Proudly brandishing their accreditation from the Southern Association of Colleges and

Schools, the same organization that green-lights schools like the University of Virginia and the College of William and Mary, Regent officials have often rebuked charges contesting their institution's academic viability by claiming that Regent is like any young university, prone to stumbling but pure in intent.

In one regard this seems sound. Regent's explosive growth over the past two decades must be on some level attributed to its appeal among success-minded conservative Christians. The university's mission has limited appeal beyond the communities that already subscribe to its perspective. If Regent meets the appropriate minimum academic standards it has every right to accreditation and its privileges.

Yet the ongoing saga of Regent School of Law, which culminated in the firing of the school's dean Herbert Titus in 1993, suggests that that which doesn't destroy the fiercely ideological university will only strengthen it.

In 1987, ABA regulators refused to grant the law school full accreditation based on a number of factors, which included insufficient faculty salaries, an inadequate law library, a part-time dean, and a paltry endowment, the *Virginian-Pilot* reported.

The ABA also challenged CBN University's version of tenure, three-year renewable contracts, arguing that a more traditional and secure form of tenure was required.

In January 1989, Titus fired off a letter to the ABA, signed by himself and Bob Slosser, then the university's president, which stated that "under no circumstances other than the ones set forth above [breach of contract or program discontinuation] would a faculty member be refused a new three-year contract on an annual basis." In effect, Titus wrote, CBN professors had tenure, and the ABA granted provisional accreditation based on that claim.

In 1993, Regent's trustees fired Titus, himself a Harvard Law School graduate, after deciding that "philosophically, Herb Titus's religious viewpoint is outside, or much narrower than that advocated or tolerated by Regent University generally," according to a report filed by ABA fact finders.

Titus's firing itself constituted a violation of Regent's tenure policy, said eight faculty members who filed a complaint with the ABA.

And so did the subsequent firing of three law professors, two of whom supposedly had tenure.

Regent had indeed violated ABA standards, stated the ABA Accreditation Committee's report released on March 17, 1995. The firings were a violation if Regent had real tenure; if the school didn't have tenure, as it had claimed in the wake of the firings, then Titus had lied all along.

At press time, Titus was in the process of suing Regent and others involved for upwards of $38 million. Included in the suit, according to Titus's attorney, Richard Kruegler of Durrett, Irvin, and Bradshaw in Richmond, Virginia, are claims of wrongful discharge, breach of contract, defamation, and conspiracy to injure his reputation. At this printing, the trial was scheduled to begin August 20, 1996.

With Titus gone, Regent implemented a new, more traditional tenure program. A month later Terry Lindvall, a young Regent film professor whose specialty was movie comedies, was named president of the university. The two events together were perceived as the beginning of the school's race to the mainstream.

Herbert Titus taught Kevin Danford's common law class, a course Danford described as revelatory. "I learned from Professor Titus that there is indeed a framework outlined Biblically for government and for law, that if you take the time to look at the Bible through a lawyer's eyes, you see a God of justice," Danford explained. "Law today is taught in schools as something that shifts and changes with the times—society is different now than it was, so law is different now than it was. The shock was to find that government has authority only within its own jurisdiction. Outside that jurisdiction—in families, churches, and businesses—it has no authority."

Even at the most basic level, a firm biblical perspective on justice would seem starkly retrograde by most Americans' standards. Looking steadfastly at the New Testament for modern legal precedent, for example, would seemingly give a society license to institute slavery (Colossians 3:22–4:1) and a death penalty for homosexuals (Romans 1:27–32).

But if Regent is educating its students properly, insurrectionist-minded graduates like Kevin Danford, who told me he hoped to run for office some day, will eventually do the bidding for a Pat Robert-son–style interpretation of bible-based law in Washington.

Robert McDonnell, a Republican from Virginia Beach and a 1989 graduate of CBN Law, was recently reelected to a second term in the Virginia General Assembly. Regent graduates also hold elected offices in the Mississippi legislature and the Baton Rouge city council in Louisiana.

John Webb, a legislative assistant to congressman Van Hilleary (Republican, Tenn.) and a 1993 graduate of Regent School of Law, was featured in a recent supplement of *Defense News* titled "Who's Who in Defense in the 104th U.S. Congressional Staff."

Another Regent graduate, Jose Gonzales, leads a Virginia Beach–based group called Semilla which mentors future Latin American leaders through Regent University, where the Uruguay-born Gonzales is an adjunct professor. Gonzales points his students, who hail from South American countries like Paraguay and Venezuela, to the Bible for instruction on building nations.

Then there's Sharon Weston, a state representative in Louisiana. A graduate of Regent's School of Communications, Weston in 1994 told the *Greater Baton Rouge Business Report,* which named her "one of the capital's rising stars," that the best advice she could give to aspiring business and community leaders was "to pray, to seek godly wisdom."

Steve Magnuson stated with pride that a friend from Regent now worked in the office of Representative William Baker (Republican, Calif.), who not surprisingly gets a 100 percent rating on the Christian Coalition's congressional scorecard. The 1994 Republican sweep in Congress no doubt provided Regent graduates with even more career possibilities on the Hill.

And at the same time Regent University is politicizing and intel-lectually arming conservative Christians, it progresses toward new frontiers in a fashion distinctly redolent of its founder's hubris.

Fall 1995 witnessed the implementation of a four-year-old Regent dream: the on-line PhD.

"The definition of a PhD program is reading, research, writing, and thinking," one Regent professor explained. "The PhD was made for the Internet and the Internet was made for the PhD."

Guided by fevered evangelical determination (and perhaps less hindered than secular academicians by obvious concerns about maintaining intellectual rigor), Regent's School of Divinity and College of Communication devised a path of doctorate study in communication "with a divinity cognate" available to students who had never even set foot in Virginia Beach.

By examining existing Internet-only graduate programs at Walden University and the University of Sarasota, Regent came up with what it claims is the first accredited remote on-line program that duplicates an existing on-campus course of study. Papers are posted using Eudora communications software; professors and students correspond via e-mail. Audio tapes of group discussion are an expected addition this year.

And plans are already in the works for the next logical step—desktop video conferencing, whereby Regent faculty will be able to see as well as hear their off-campus pupils.

For many years, Robertson's biggest obstacle in growing Regent was financial solubility. Four years ago Robertson gave the university a $117 million endowment from the CBN coffers. Much of the endowment came in the form of investment securities which Regent later sold for $107.5 million and reinvested. Added expenses—the new investments underperformed and the university tipped $9 million out of the endowment to finance the new law building—forced layoffs in 1995, including the school's registrar and vice president for finance and operations.

All of which dovetails with another brilliant aspect of Regent's "innovative" cyber-degree, one which ought to send Robertson skeptics reeling. Although tuition for the on-line PhD program—which could be argued is nothing more than a glorified correspondence course—is the same as if one attended classes in person, the cost to the university is substantially diminished.

"The hard place to bring this together is the radical religious dimension and the belief in the gifts of the Holy Spirit, healing, some of the radical prophetic theology that Pat Robertson drifts in and out of," said David Edwin Harrell Jr. "Most of us at some point in the religious dialogue that goes on will think that we've gotten pretty far out on the fringe. So the outsider's reaction is, well, this must be a pretty irrational environment, whereas in truth in almost every other way what goes on there is like what goes on, on any conservative college campus."

—◦—

If Regent University is Pat Robertson's best shot at exerting influence on the minds of tomorrow, then the American Center for Law and Justice is his swipe at the minds of today.

Started by Robertson in 1991 as a public-interest law firm fashioned after the American Civil Liberties Union, the ACLJ has since staked its ground as the most visible religious-rights legal action group in the country.

"Back in the early eighties, I took a long look at what the civil liberties union was doing to take religion from the public square of America," Robertson told *The New York Times.* "It was like an all-out vendetta against religious values. There didn't seem like there was any champion to stand up against them."

Since then executive director Keith Fournier and chief counsel Jay Sekulow have led the ACLJ into some of the nation's highest-profile battles over topics such as abortion, prayer in schools, and public displays of religion.

When Pat Robertson first met Sekulow in 1990, the Atlanta-based lawyer had already established himself in the field with his own firm, Christian Advocates Serving Evangelism. "Pat knew of my work," Sekulow told me, "he had supported it, and said he was thinking about starting a law center to combat what he perceived to be a very orchestrated attack on religious liberty and he asked me if I would consider joining."

Sekulow proved to be one of Robertson's most estimable hires. Raised in a conservative Jewish household in Brooklyn, New York, Sekulow converted to Christianity as a young man and attended college and law school at Mercer University, a Baptist-affiliated school in Atlanta. Easygoing and loquacious, Sekulow has also played a part in many of the landmark religious cases of the past decade.

"I had taken a number of cases before the Supreme Court, one of which Pat had helped fund," said Sekulow, referring to *Board of Edu-*

cation of Westside Community Schools v. Mergens, the case that authorized Bible clubs in public schools. In another, settled in 1987, Sekulow defended the organization Jews for Jesus.

While smaller legal groups devoted to defending public expressions of religious faith, like the Rutherford Institute and the Christian Legal Society Center for Law and Religious Freedom, had been in existence before the ACLJ, none possessed the kind of financial and organizational muscle Robertson could provide.

The ACLJ has a budget of $12 million and employs a staff of 15 lawyers, plus 500 "affiliates" who consult on specific cases in all 50 states. Sekulow estimated the center has from 300,000 to 500,000 donors.

"And this effort was focused on pro-liberty, pro-life, and pro-family work," Sekulow explained, "in the courtrooms and through educational efforts, and that was the primary focus; it wasn't part of something bigger."

With its increased success, the ACLJ has divided into "projects," task forces devoted to specific areas, such as religious liberties, family life, human life, economic liberty, minority empowerment, and education.

Sekulow acknowledged the center's debt to its 75-year-old nemesis. "The American Civil Liberties Union was our best prototype," he said. "We took a lot of plays off their playbook." The ACLJ not only aped the civil liberties group's organizational structure but its aggressive courtroom posture.

The American Center for Law and Justice claims it defends religious free speech for everyone, not just Christians, because "if one person's rights are denied, it affects everyone," said Sekulow, who once defended the Hare Krishnas before the Supreme Court.

ACLJ triumphs in high-profile Supreme Court cases like *Lamb's Chapel v. Center Moriches Union School District,* which concerned a church that wanted to use a public school facility in the evening to show a "family values" film; and *Rosenberger v. The University of Virginia,* where the court ruled for the first time in favor of a public school subsidizing a religious activity, have enabled the firm in some cases to successfully portray itself as a liberty-minded maverick, out to defend the constitutional rights of those with unpopular religious beliefs.

By firmly grounding religious expression within the realm of free speech, rather than free exercise, the ACLJ painted religious conservatives as progressives. In the Lamb's Chapel case, the ACLU even filed a brief in support of the ACLJ position.

"The easy thing to have done would have been modeling like every other Christian religious liberties group, but we cut a new path in that regard," Sekulow said, "and Pat gave us the freedom to do it."

The American Center for Law and Justice, like Regent University, has made headway by diverting attention from its controversial perspective and instead focusing the debate on increasing the civil rights of all Americans. Critics argue that this is a subtly specious approach which fails to acknowledge that expanding one group's rights almost always abridges another's.

A good example is the role the ACLJ has played in the courtrooms in regard to abortion. The center has defended Randall Terry, the founder of the antiabortion group Operation Rescue, in cases concerning protests outside abortion clinics and contested the legality of "bubble zones" that keep protests at certain distances outside those clinics.

The end effect is that opinions that have long existed outside the farthest-flung parameters of an issue's center stage are instantly reeled back within its borders. Whether the ACLJ is a moderating influence protecting people of faith from their mortal enemies or a troublesomely brilliant practitioner of litigious role reversal depends on where one's political perspective lies.

"I want to see people of faith, Christians in particular, not denied access to the marketplace of ideas, not treated as second-class citizens, and not afraid to talk about their faith or a Biblical worldview in that marketplace," said Sekulow, "with the ultimate goal that the view of Christians on the cultural issues of the day will not just be tolerated but welcomed with anticipation."

Sekulow's seditious brio is as good a gauge as any of the ACLJ's progress so far. "One of the best compliments I ever got," he said, "was from one of the lawyers at the National Organization for Women, who said we were so dangerous because we sounded so reasonable."

CHAPTER THIRTEEN

❖

The 700 Club,
April 9, 1991, 10:00 A.M.

This is really not something you want your children to be watching, but we know that you would want to know about it," says an attractive but heavily made-up woman with an oblong, eggplant-shaped head, cotton-candy hair, and a Scottish accent. "Abortion, sex literature, contraceptives, they provide it all to anyone who asks, including your teenager. 'They' are, of course, Planned Parenthood." Today's central topic on *The 700 Club* is a familiar Robertson jeremiad. The interlocutor is Sheila Walsh, a successful "contemporary Christian" singer who joined the *700 Club* as a cohost from 1988 to 1992. "It's absolutely revolting that Planned Parenthood entices these young people in from the malls, from the streets, and then promotes abortion to the hilt." That's an unidentified man, clean-cut and casually dressed, being interviewed outside a Planned Parenthood facility in Chesapeake, Virginia. The "newsmagazine" segment of the story has begun rolling, and this initial clip serves to clarify the piece's point of view from the start. A female voice-over (Walsh identified the unseen correspondent as Andrea Francis) explains that the Planned Parenthood clinic targets teenagers, as a close-up of an advertisement placed in a local paper, which reads "Special Prices for Students: Bring This Ad in For $5.00 Off the Initial Exam." The next image is a wide shot of four protesters, including the still unnamed male, another man, a woman, and a preteen girl, standing outside of a modern three-floor office building, waving placards that read "Choose Life." They are all chanting but they appear to have no adversaries. Narrator Francis says that the clinic's placement "across the street" from a mall is

195

proof that Planned Parenthood is promoting abortion among teens. From what the viewer can see, though, the name Planned Parenthood is not emblazoned anywhere on the building's exterior. And the next shot reveals that the "street" that divides Planned Parenthood from the mall (seen at middle distance) looks more like a four-lane highway. Another glimpse at the picketers shows a more convincing group of twenty or so neatly dressed men and women brandishing signs at the sidewalk. A young woman in a flower-print summer dress with a conspicuously high neckline complains to her interviewer that Planned Parenthood abrogates her rights as parent, by offering to "do the job for you." From here, the feature continues on pretty much how you might expect. A representative from a group called the Christian Action Council says during a behind-his-desk interview that he opposes Planned Parenthood's practice of distributing sex-education literature confidentially to anyone who asks for it. He adds, "They will say, the law guarantees confidentiality, which is true." One fascinating trend I notice as I'm watching the broadcast is how the coverage weaves in and out of objectivity as the footage rolls on. The reporter says that Planned Parenthood distributes literature that encourages teens to decide for themselves about sex and describes different sexual practices, "from oral sex to bestiality," without judging them. I suspect that most of this is true, at least the stuff about deciding for oneself and the nonjudgmental tone. Then the report visits with Connie Youngkin, a mother in San Diego, who tells the story of how she went to a Planned Parenthood office and requested materials to help her explain sex to her 12-year-old daughter. They handed her a hip but frank book titled *Changing Bodies, Changing Lives* by Ruth Bell and coauthors, that is included on the Planned Parenthood recommended reading list. Presuming that teenagers irresponsible enough to have unprotected sex are motivated enough to chase down recommended readings, they will find (the pages are shown on screen as proof) sections titled "Sex With Yourself," "Exploring Sex With Someone Else," and "Exploring Sex With Someone of Your Own Sex." The voice-over continues, "The authors tell teens that, 'As far as we're concerned, the only time any sex is perverted or immoral is if it is being forced on someone.' " Youngkin explains how the authors characterized oral and anal sex as acceptable forms of sexual intercourse, even suggesting teens "might like the smells in the liquid. . . ." Now, I don't happen to have any problems with any of this; but I can appreciate why some conservative Christians might. I also respect anybody's right to pursue the ideals they believe in, including backing legislation to prevent others from engaging in practices they deem improper. These are basic political ground rules, no more and no less. It's when these hard kernels of truth get candy-coated with sweet ideological nuggets that matters get sticky. Youngkin herself seems clearly and genuinely offended by the degree of sexual detail within. And to add insult to injury, she says that when she complained to Planned Parenthood, she was called "old-fashioned" (although why that would be an insult to someone who embraces 1950s values, I'm not sure). The only problem is that none of this has much to do with the story's original premise, that Planned Parenthood allegedly lures teenagers into their clinics and preaches abortion.

———◇———

For the next segment, *The 700 Club* resorts to sending two 16-year-old girls to a Planned Parenthood clinic after the organization reportedly refused to grant CBN News an on-camera interview. The counselor reputedly educated the girls about birth control, using terms such as mutual masturbation and oral sex, and demonstrated how to use a condom. According to the report, and tattooed across the screen in bold white letters, she also advised them that "the decision to have sex was a personal one, and urged them to be responsible, use contraceptives and 'you won't get pregnant, you won't get any diseases, and no one ever has to know.' " Maybe you're wondering what I'm wondering: If the information was so potentially damaging to teens, why was it appropriate for CBN News to send two 16-year-old girls to Planned Parenthood to obtain it? The report returns to Connie Youngkin in her living room and Mr. Christian Action Council in his office—who both essentially reconfirm that they disapprove the distribution of *any* materials that explicate safe sex to teenagers. (How will 13-year-olds, who can't even remember to clean up their bedrooms, argues Mr. CAC, remember to take the Pill every day?) In the next shot our two blonde-girl sleuths are being interviewed outdoors, seated at a cement picnic table, by an unidentified curly-haired woman whose back is turned to the camera. The voice-over explains that "the Planned Parenthood counselor also told the girls, if their parents didn't understand, don't talk to them about it." In an ultra-close-up of one pink-faced youth (she and her friend are never identified by name), she says, "It's not necessary to tell them at all, that you shouldn't even tell your friends or anybody, that you should just keep it between you and your boyfriend." The other girl, whose face is a little rounder and even pinker, adds, "They just said basically that our parents wouldn't understand and parents just don't understand." For the next shot, the camera shows the two teens leaving the Planned Parenthood clinic, smiling and chatting. In the last shot of the segment, Andrea Francis finally appears on screen, outdoors on somebody's front lawn. She looks to be in her mid-twenties, suited in conservative gray flannel with a couple strings of pearls around her neck. Francis tells the camera that studies have revealed that when teenagers are involved in programs which emphasize abstinence, the teen pregnancy rate decreases but when teenagers are given access to contraceptives through family-planning clinics, the teen pregnancy rate escalates. "Still, Planned Parenthood has publicly criticized chastity programs," she says, "leaving many parents wondering what Planned Parenthood has to gain by pushing teenagers to become sexually active. I'm Andrea Francis, CBN News."

————————⟨o⟩————————

As with most CBN news updates, *The 700 Club* report on Planned Parenthood leans heavily to the right while most of its facts appear reasonably accurate. CBN is ostensibly providing a service for conservative Christians. In *Politically Incorrect*, Ralph Reed alludes to a 1993 survey done by the conservative Media Research Center that the major networks offered "statistically insignificant coverage of religion." Reed writes that, of those scant religious features, "many . . . treated religion in the context of pathology and violence: sexual abuse by Catholic priests, acts of vandalism committed against abortion clinics, the bombing of the World Trade Center by Islamic terrorists, and the shooting of abortionists." This makes sense. In the same way that tabloid TV shows like *Hard Copy* and *Extra!* are drawn toward celebrity scandals and that your local evening newscast hones in on crime stories, the networks tend to level their heaviest blows at powerful individuals or institutions. Viewers want their own anxieties reinforced. If crime is a growing concern, it's only natural that news of illegal activity draws attention. Similarly, the growing economic class divide fosters interest in the foibles of the rich or famous. Watchers of *The 700 Club* no doubt fear the erosion of religious morals in the public sphere. For most of them, Planned Parenthood is probably already viewed as a leftist talisman. In a capitalist society, if there's a viable market for a particular point of view, that market deserves to be serviced. There's nothing inherently dishonest about offering to marinate someone's brain in the vinaigrette of their choice. What is more interesting to watch is when the feature returns for a visit with the Reverend–Not Reverend and the argument goes beyond routine television tautology.

————◁◦▷————

We're back in the studio with Pat Robertson and Sheila Walsh, side by side in cloth-upholstered armchairs. A mammoth bank of serious-looking control boards glows behind them. Using one of his favorite rhetorical devices, Robertson takes the part of the mild-mannered pedagogue while the demure Sheila Walsh plays the insatiable student. "You talk in your book *The New Millennium*—" ventures Walsh, palpably swallowing a lump in her throat as she engages the master. "—I remember you talked about Margaret Sanger, about the origins and the agenda of Planned Parenthood. When I watched that story, it almost seems to me as if they've gone away from her agenda, it seems as if they're encouraging free sex, where she was talking about sterilization and all sorts of stuff." "Well, just the opposite," says Robertson, his gentle voice gurgling up like mountain spring water. "This *is* part of her agenda." He labels Sanger "really weird" and then explains how, during her lifetime, the founder of Planned Parenthood encouraged her granddaughter to have sex at least three times a day and had numerous adulterous affairs. "Her main thrust was toward what's called eugenics," Robertson continues. "She wrote a pamphlet in

1924, *Breeding the Thoroughbred,* and she said, We must take away from the gene pool the defective ones." "That's like Adolf Hitler!" Walsh exclaims, her head cocked in apparent disbelief. "Hitler copied her," says Robertson. "Oh, really?" Walsh swoons. "Hitler copied one of the key members of the Planned Parenthood organization was a doctor whose writings were copied by Hitler [*sic*]. But you ask yourself, who are the defectives?" "Well, who would they be?" asks Walsh with a nervous giggle. "Well, you and me, for starters," Robertson comes back. "Why?" Walsh says, looking truly amazed. "Well, because we're fundamentalist Christians, we'd have to be crazy." Walsh stifles a slight and disbelieving laugh as she straightens herself in her seat. "So who else would come under that?" she says. "Southern Europeans—Italians, Spaniards, Portuguese." "What, they're supposed to be lazy?" Walsh asks. "No, they're just defective by her standards. And then mentally defective people and all their relatives—" "How could that ever be implemented?" Walsh tries to interrupt. But Robertson is on a roll. "—And blacks. Blacks are defective. And Jews. So she wanted to sterilize all of those people. That was her agenda. And she sold the big think tanks: She got 50 million, I think, from the Rockefeller interests; she got 50 million from the Ford Foundation. . . ." What's fascinating here is how gracefully Robertson allows his impressively collated string of supposedly salubrious truths about Sanger to deteriorate into a torrent of logorrhea. Sanger *did* have numerous affairs, including legendary ones with H. G. Wells and Havelock Ellis, she *did* encourage women to have sex for reasons other than procreation, and she *did* flirt with the intellectual fad known as eugenics in the 1910s, as did many progressives of her day. But in truth, Sanger only ever entertained two points of eugenic thought: 1) Severely retarded people (persons with a mental age of about eight, she said) should not bear children; and 2) unlimited childbearing in large families increased the possibility of raising children of lower intelligence. Sanger expressly counseled against race-based eugenics. By 1919 Sanger had written the following in the *Birth Control Review:* "We maintain that a woman possessing an adequate knowledge of her reproductive functions is the best judge of time and conditions under which her child should be brought into the world. We maintain that it is her right, regardless of all other considerations, to determine whether she shall bear children or not, and how many children she shall bear if she chooses to. . . ." A 1992 article in *The National Review* even convincingly argued that the Sanger-founded *Birth Control Review* occasionally provided a platform for racist thinkers like Ernst Rudin, Hitler's director of sterilization, who published there in April 1933. Little of this has anything to do with the issue at hand, which is Planned Parenthood's alleged proselytizing. But by now Robertson simply can't help himself. ". . . What she wanted to do first was get everybody having sex as much as they could," continues Robertson, turning toward Walsh as he folds up his page of notes, "then she was going to introduce abortion, because that wasn't popular . . . they wanted to start birth control, then abortion, then when they had so many babies they couldn't control it they wanted to start sterilization. . . ." In February 1988, while running for president, Pat Robertson went before a New Hampshire legislative committee studying the state's abortion laws and stated that Planned Parenthood's long-range goal was to create a "master race." At the time, Faye Wattleton, then the head of the Planned Parenthood Federation of America, called the allegations "unfounded and, frankly, ridiculous." As for Margaret Sanger, Wattleton added, her "philosophies were not based on eugenics—her philosophy was based on people being allowed to choose for themselves." And here, four years later, on today's *700 Club,* the onslaught continues: ". . . What Planned Parenthood is doing is absolutely contrary to everything Christian," Robertson says, punctuating each point with his clenched fingers. "It is teaching kids to fornicate, teaching people to have adultery, teaching people to get involved in every kind of bestiality, homosexuality, lesbianism, everything that the Bible condemned." Hate speech this pure is no doubt hard to justify, even within the attenuated confines of what is today's ultraconservative Christian movement. Robertson seems to realize this as he expertly guides his diatribe in for a smooth landing. "Now folks, you say, they're free, and I think they're free to say anything they want to," Robertson says, allowing his suspended eyebrows to give way to a guileless smirk as the camera comes in for a close-up. "I'm free to say what I jolly well please, and I don't agree with this bunch of people. But that's my opinion, and they've got their opinion, so in a free society we talk about it. But I don't get any government money, but they do." Robertson explains that Planned Parenthood received over 30 million taxpayer dollars in 1991. "Now *that's* what I don't like." So write to the Energy & Commerce Committee in Washington, Robertson advises, and tell them you don't want to support Margaret Sanger's plan to "sterilize Jews and blacks and mental defectives." He adds, nonsensically, "If she tries to get to me, she's too late, I've already got nine grandchildren."

———◁○▷———

Frightened by this Planned Parenthood report, viewers of *The 700 Club* may well have written to Washington to protest federally funded sex education programs. But were they aware that they were simultaneously lobbying in favor of Robertson's business interests? In 1991, the Family Channel's 1990 income tax return was still under examination by the IRS, which had questioned the legality of funneling tax-exempt CBN funds into the for-profit Family Channel. By 1994, the IRS had settled amicably with International Family Entertainment, the Family Channel's corporate parent. (The IRS is under no obligation to produce such closing agreements, unless it decides to take the entity in question to court.) It's a tribute to Robertson's artful dodging that his business interests are buried so deeply with this TV feature. While *700 Club* viewers might do well to question the ethics of Pat Robertson's behavior in this instance, it's hard to deny him his exactitude. I must admit feeling flummoxed on some level by this program's Möbius-strip construction; I suspect I'm not the only one.

———◁○▷———

In an interesting coda, Sheila Walsh (aka Sheila Walsh Miller; Sheila Walsh Pfaehler) vanished from her post as *700 Club* cohost in August 1992, without explanation. On November 2, 1992, Walsh reappeared with a more subdued haircut, as a guest, alongside Robertson and her soon-to-be replacement Terry Meeuwsen to explain. ". . . I did some really bizarre things," Walsh said. "In July, I left my home, I left my husband. . . . I had a breakdown and I ended up in a Christian clinic for a month. And it was kind of crazy, to go from one day being on

The 700 Club, where they do your hair nice and your makeup and clothes, to checking into what effectively was a psychiatric ward, where they took my hair dryer and my makeup away—you know, in case I hurt myself. Where I wandered around in a bathrobe—where I was reduced to nothing." It was Walsh's last live appearance on *The 700 Club.*

———◦———

By the way, Robertson was correct about the federal funding of Planned Parenthood: The national organization received $37 million in 1991. What the Reverend–Not Reverend neglected to mention was that this amount was but a small fraction of the $150 million in federal funds appropriated that year for the nation's family planning program.

CHAPTER FOURTEEN

The Main Event

O n the evening of March 23, 1996, the Saturday before the Academy Awards, a thousand formally dressed revelers rode the down escalator into the bejeweled bowels of the wing-shaped Century Plaza Hotel in Los Angeles. Onlookers might easily have mistaken the well-heeled, largely silver-haired crowd for attendees at a lavish, pre-Oscar bash. Out front a white Rolls Royce vied with black stretch limousines in the circular driveway that less than two weeks earlier had delivered the distinctly more Hollywood (read: liberal) likes of Annette Bening, Michael Douglas, Michael J. Fox, and Richard Dreyfuss to a dinner honoring, paradoxically, the presentation of the ACLU's Torch of Liberty award to director Rob Reiner.

As I descended by escalator into the reception area, I understood that tonight, too, the stars would twinkle. Beneath a regal gabled ceiling dripping in gold leaf, an oddly matched group of celebrities—big and not-so-big—including Pat Boone, Jane Russell, George Foreman, and not one but two cast members of the forgotten '80s sitcom *Facts of Life,* held court in various corners of the room. Men in tuxedos escorting women in crinoline promenaded their way into the chandeliered grand ballroom to the big-band stylings of the Ralph Carmichael Orchestra.

Here there was scant evidence of the people who formed the "low-budget, no-frills, volunteer driven, high-tech groups [that] packed grassroots punch with blazing efficiency and little overhead" which Ralph Reed has claimed represent today's "pro-family movement."

This was the Pat Robertson Roast, a glitzy fifties-style extravaganza of blissfully Robertsonesque proportions, concocted to serve the dueling purposes of sending up the boss on his sixty-sixth birthday and drumming up funds for Regent University. So maybe this was how things used to be in Hollywood, I thought—when it was the Rat Pack not the Brat Pack and matinee idols were worth idolizing.

As the Martinelli's sparkling cider, chilled in silver buckets at each table in lieu of champagne, began flowing, I thought again, maybe not.

I came to the roast on a tip that CNN talk show host Larry King would be master of ceremonies. Truth is, King's participation, at first a disorienting touch, made the evening bearably entertaining, even by conventional standards.

Opening remarks were made by Terry Lindvall, president of Regent University, and former Los Angeles police commissioner Bert Boeckmann, philanthropist and the owner of the Van Nuys–based Galpin Motors, one of the largest car dealerships in the country.

When Rabbi Daniel Lapin, a well-bespoken bearded man who wears a skullcap on his balding pate, blessed the proceedings in a clipped British accent, matters began to come into focus.

"Every time Pat Robertson and I are in the same room, the *New York Times* takes interest," joked Lapin, this night an apparent exception. Then, with more gusto, as he beamed upon Robertson and his wife seated at the head of the center table at the stage's apron, Lapin said, "There are two kinds of people in the world, Pat and Dede and the rest of us."

Regent donors had paid a minimum of $500 a head to dine on flame-grilled petit filet mignon with gourmet mushrooms, shallots, and thyme butter and Australian cold water lobster tail with scallion lemon sauce, while mixing with the celebrities placed at each table.

Seated at mine was an attractive black actress, hair piled on her head, Alaina Reed Hall, who is featured on the Warner Brothers sitcom *Cleghorne!* Hall said she had never met Pat Robertson but had allowed *The 700 Club* to visit her house and videotape her born-again testimony.

"I'm here for the meal," she declaimed to the table with a brassy snort. "They send the car and I come."

Her companion, a short-haired African-American woman in her late thirties who once sang backup for Stevie Wonder and Philip Bailey, told me she grew up Catholic in Minnesota, had once been a member of the Church on the Way, and that she respected Pat Robertson very much because he "had given so much."

As a white-uniformed waitstaff served custard pastries twirled like tulips and decaffeinated coffee, a dark-suited pianist with a rooster's crest of jet-black hair played "Unforgettable" and "Let My People Go" in a rococo-lite manner, backed by a soaring prerecorded string section and choir that suggested he was channeling Liberace. Lou Rawls sang "Wind Beneath My Wings," fixing his gaze on Robertson every time he repeated the line "Did you ever know that you're my hero?" Rawls wrapped things up with his signature "You'll Never Find," kicking out his right leg in classic Vegas fashion as his gold cuff-flinks gave up sparkle to the spotlight.

"Jesus Christ, this has been a long night!" barked Larry King into the center mike as a hint of stale, nervous sweat wafted over the crowd.

"You're an American rabbi?" King added, fingering the Seattle-based Lapin in the audience. "I don't believe it. I never heard an American rabbi who talks like you."

King in person was a taller, more imposing version of his TV self. The larger-than-life effect kept King in good stead when his more biting remarks were met with a sour mixture of overly hearty guffaws and genuine squawks of horror from the audience.

King sat Robertson to his left, in mock *Larry King Live* fashion, bravely shooting most of the zingers that the other roasters didn't dare to even set in their crosshatches. King's most pointed one-liners suggested that Pat Robertson wants everybody's money, that Pat Robertson thinks he's God, and that Pat Robertson is an extreme right-winger. Of course, he was just kidding.

King's role, whether he realized it or not, was clearly that of "show Jew," a term Frank Rich once coined to describe a familiar brand of token guest at Robertson events, whose presence is most effective if he happens to be famous and openly disagrees with Pat.

The juxtaposition was a seamless one, though. Within minutes, King was hunched over an oversize microphone, jacket off, his bow tie dangling from his open collar, whereas Robertson kept buttoned-up, with a silver crucifix discreetly pinned below his black tie.

"Pat, we've always admired how cool and calm you are under fire from the press," went a typical King jab. "Ronald Reagan may have been our Teflon president, but you are 100 percent asbestos."

Beyond the obvious inconsistencies of the patter—that the analogy doesn't scan, that Robertson never was president—was its peculiar structure. King's material had a funny way of revealing truths and yet, by putting them in the form of jokes, rendering those same truths silly-sounding and trivial.

Over the course of the evening, Rosy Grier and George Foreman did a comedy routine; former *Saturday Night Live* cast member Victoria Jackson, ukulele in tow, chirped a would-be campaign song called "Pat Robertson, Where Are You?" to the tune of the theme from *Car 54, Where Are You?;* and bodybuilder and fitness expert Jake Steinfeld (Body By Jake) called Robertson a "mensch."

"I grew up wearing Calvin Klein jeans," quipped the super-tan supermodel Kim Alexis, awkwardly scanning a TelePrompTer, "you grew up with Calvin Coolidge."

Even more entertaining than trying to reimagine each celebrity roaster now that I knew they presumably were either conservative or Christian enough to cuddle up to Robertson's controversial image were the out-of-character videotaped greetings that appeared intermittently on two giant stage-side screens. Jerry Falwell's, for example, was genuinely funny, George Bush's was irksomely buddy-buddy, and Rush Limbaugh's was unexpectedly irreverent. In another clip, comedian Fred Travelena did impressions of well-known religious personalities.

An elderly white couple from Cleveland sat opposite me at my table. The wife asked Alaina Reed Hall whether she knew the actress who played Mrs. Jefferson on the old *Jeffersons* sitcom, acted disappointed when she said she didn't, and then proceeded down a list of other black celebrities.

Every half hour, it seemed, the husband would yell across to me and ask where I was from. When I'd answer New York the conversation would stop short, but then he'd ask me again a little bit later as if I might eventually come up with a more palatable answer.

Back onstage, a dead-on Bill Clinton impersonator did a funnier and fairer parody than I would have expected (e.g., very few Hillary jokes) which had Robertson in stitches.

The fact is, the motley aggregate of celebrities added a pleasantly kitschy air to the evening. For example, Chuck Woolery, once the squeaky-clean host of the deliciously seamy *Love Connection* TV game show, drew admirers in a shadow at the side of the room, thus an otherwise innocuous personality found himself bathed in a mysterious, phosphorescent glow. (Woolery had recently signed on to the cast of *Home & Family,* a new Family Channel morning chat show. His cohost was Christina Ferrare, the former model who just happens to be married to MTM head Tony Thomopoulos.)

Out in the lobby after the show, a velvet-slippered Wink Martindale, game show host nonpareil, excitedly posed guests for photos with the Clinton look-alike.

What was it about aging game show hosts? Did Robertson somehow provide these purveyors of rhinestoned fantasy from another, more naïve era with a promise of real-life parity? Maybe it's just that he keeps them gainfully employed.

This "through the looking-glass" journey worked both ways, it occurred to me. Larry King repeatedly kidding Ben Kinchlow about his puffball coif—calling it the "strangest-looking hair I've ever seen," as if it had made the *700 Club* regular as famous as Don King— couldn't conceal the fact that King had no idea before this night who the heck this guy, whom he had minutes earlier mistakenly introduced as "Ken Kinchlow," was.

Similarly, former *700 Club* cohost Sheila Walsh, virtually unrecognizable to even her former viewers in a new upswept blond hairstyle, crooned a barely credible Broadway show tune called "That's Pat" to her former employer. No one lesser than Julie Andrews, never mind a second-rate gospel singer, could have delivered with such a tepid number anywhere else and still expected to receive the generous applause Walsh did.

Other pretaped video segments cast Pat Robertson in equally improbable pop-culture roles. One was a reel of Robertson bloopers from *The 700 Club;* another compiled clips of Robertson doing silly things like jumping rope in the form of a TV-commercial lampoon from "Pray-Tel Records" for *Pat Robertson's Greatest Hits.*

The most bizarre was a film parody that placed Pat Robertson at the center of an Oliver Stone feature called *Robertson.* The low-resolution black-and-white short, the least clever of the three, starred an actor who looked nothing like Robertson skulking around and intimidating people. Again Robertson was being portrayed as a mass-media icon, someone of such historical consequence that he had transcended criticism, so much so that he had become an object worthy of both reification and scorn.

Even Robertson's son, Tim, joined in. After praising his father for instilling in him family values and an unerring faith in God, the 38-year-old president of International Family Entertainment made fun of his father's programming skills. He told the crowd that Pat Robertson had come up with the idea for *Friends* first, except he had cast a Quaker in the lead role; likewise for *E.R.*, except in Robertson's proposal the title stood for "extreme right."

Robertson's comedic transmutation was so complete that by the time Jay Sekulow made remarks that seemed overly pious and reverential, and hence totally out of synch with the rest of the evening's jocular tone, Larry King was moved to ad-lib, "That's a very serious man," as the ACLJ's chief counsel exited.

In the annals of Hollywood parties, the Pat Robertson Roast was truly the Stealth bomber of entertainment events: a gala high-profile enough to assure its attendees that they had attended a momentously potent gathering of Tinsel Town's most righteous movers and shakers that somehow remained absolutely invisible to everyone else, leaving not even a bleep on the mainstream press's radar screen. Unless you had been personally invited, you would have to have been a faithful *700 Club* viewer to have even heard about the event.

Finally, Pat Robertson took to the center mike and gave bland thanks to everyone for coming out to support Regent University. It was Dr. Jack Hayford, pastor of the Church on the Way, that asked for everyone to join hands at their tables and pray along.

——————<○>——————

Within the preceding pages, I've attempted to map out the parameters of Pat Robertson's universe, including even its outermost regions. I have done this armed with the belief that, in his effort to sell mainstream society on a value system too extreme for its tastes, Pat Robertson has become an exemplar for how one might manipulate and coordinate the powerful tools and techniques of communication that modernity has devised in order to steer a culture.

I do not intend this book to be some sort of clarion call, alerting the unwitting citizens of an impending threat to freedom. For one, to shift the American culture so radically away from its current course toward plurality and progress I think would be an outlandishly difficult task for one person, even one as resourceful as Pat Robertson.

So what? Having read this far into this book you might still find cause to pose this question.

So what if Pat Robertson and his ideas have infiltrated the American mainstream? So what if he has built a utopian microcosm of the world the way he sees it? So what if he preaches intolerance: Americans have an unalienable right to believe what they want to believe, don't they? So what if the world Pat Robertson has imagined is simply a cleaner, more Christian adjunct of the real one? So what if Pat Robertson has made millions selling people something they want to buy?

Even researcher Jonathan Hudson, a harsh Robertson critic, admitted to me during an interview, "When you look at the operation of International Family Entertainment, the business simply functions like any other media empire."

That is, corporations deliver exactly what their customers demand: more of the same. It's a given among entertainment media types that television and movies done right means spoon-feeding each demographic a freshly mushed-up version of the same flavor pabulum it responded to once before.

Critics at the dawn of the television age used to whine about how the "boob tube" was blanding out American culture and erasing precious regional distinctions. All it takes is a little expedient cross-country travel today to discover that this particular prophecy never came true. Just because substantial groups of TV viewers in New Orleans, Tulsa, and Butte, Montana, are enjoying *Seinfeld* each week doesn't mean they behave any more like neurotic New York Jews than their forebears.

Likewise, generation after generation of audiences might take to the homespun Americana of *The Waltons,* even as each subsequent generation's fragmented lives bear an ever-fading resemblance to the tightly knit family structure portrayed on the show.

Television relies on superficiality, not verisimilitude. Bill McKibben, in his book *The Age of Missing Information,* observed that television "more or less takes us into its confidence—it says, 'You know it's silly to be watching Donna Reed reruns after thirty-five years, and we know it's silly. That's why we're packaging them this funny way, with lots of jokes about how silly she is living in her "dream house" and so on.' What it doesn't say is, once you're swelled with this agreeable sense of your hip superiority, you can be sold products as easily as a tribesman just emerging from the bush."

And television can make any subject seem superficial. Consider MTV, the premier youth-culture cable channel. Although it makes loads of gestures toward subversiveness (loud music, outrageous clothes, *Beavis & Butt-head*), it is no more or less reassuring than everything else on television. Even PBS, TV's last bastion of noncommercial culture, seems much more about its trappings (classical music, *Masterpiece Theater,* and telethons) than its unlikely premise, that all "good" television resides there.

Bill McKibben also wrote that "TV retains its power because it's trained us not to take it seriously." In 1985, Tim Robertson, then CBN's head of programming, betrayed his father's unique understanding of that power, telling an industry trade paper, "I don't know that television *should* be just like life. Maybe television should hold up something a little bit better." Describing CBN's dramatic fare, Robertson added, "These are shows that say you can be a good person and still be a winner. You can win. That's essentially the message of Christianity: You can win."

All this from a guy whose job it is to secure 30-second ad spots.

———◁◇▷———

It was only a matter of time before somebody got the idea to apply the entertainment industry's finely honed subterfuge techniques to sell a worldview instead of inanimate consumer goods.

While The Family Channel lulls you into familiar TV territory with favorite old reruns and the promise of inoffensive "pro-family" programming the whole family can enjoy, Pat Robertson can ostensibly force-feed his conservative evangelical agenda.

By playing into people's better instincts—that (of course) we're in dire need of a wholesome antidote to shock TV—Robertson invites his viewers to let down their guard. Once convinced that The Family Channel's superficial version of family values is suitably reassuring, some of those viewers—particularly those who strongly identify themselves as Christian—will be drawn to Robertson's kindly visage and conversant perspective.

"Leaders like Pat Robertson have sold the people that I call Paul and Patty Pew-Warmer, sitting out in the pews there on Sundays, on a few really good ideas," said Jerry Sloan, who heads Project Tocsin, a Sacramento-based group that monitors the religious right in California. "That abortion is wrong, that we've got to drive the Sodomites from the land, that we need to get prayer back in schools, ideas like that. And you've got Paul and Patty sitting out there hearing their preacher Sunday after Sunday and Wednesday night after Wednesday night that America ought to be a Christian country. And they have never stopped to think of the consequences of what happens. Okay, we're a Christian country, now what happens?

"R. J. Rushdoony said that all societies separate and segregate," Sloan continued. "Of course if you give any faith a preferred status, then all others are separated for progressive elimination. So there are only three ways to carry out progressive elimination: one, you convert people; two, you drive them out of the country; three, you kill them."

Knowing full well that the fiercest, most unpalatable rendition of his Weltanschauung could never sustain a top-notch operation, Robertson the pragmatist opts for Pyrrhic victories.

If he can't get a majority to see it all his way, he can certainly construct new diversions in an attempt to convince different segments of the population that he's their man long enough that they might donate to his cause. Not coincidentally, the segment of the population most vulnerable to Robertson's pitches is the one in which he first found support: evangelical Christians.

In 1990, CBN started an organization to sell home Bible-study courses; within two years Robertson had signed off on a plan to transform the operation into an independent for-profit company that sold "passport" books, filled with discount coupons for various products, from health supplements to vacation properties.

Targeted specifically to evangelical Christians, the firm, which at alternate times was called American Benefits Plus and American Sales Corporation, was structured on multilevel marketing principles that Robertson had derived from the Bible.

Independent distributors were employed and instructed to recruit their friends as subdistributors. Commissions were collected by each tier of distributors from the tier below them.

Over 20,000 Robertson supporters joined up as distributors in the first year, frequently shelling out their own money to purchase promotional fliers and videos created to promote the company. Within a year a Beverly Hills fitness entrepreneur named Jim Heflin had convinced Robertson to make a line of vitamin products—manufactured by Heflin—the company's main product.

Soon the company, co-owned by CBN and Pat Robertson, had changed its name to KaloVita, The Good Life Co., and began promoting merchandise such as a nutritional drink called American Whey and a Sea of Galilee line of skin-care products.

Only after Robertson fired KaloVita's president Mark Peterson in 1992 did the bottom drop out of the troubled startup. Peterson later confessed in interviews with *Newsweek* magazine and ABC News that he believed KaloVita's vitamins to be dangerously potent and obscenely overpriced. "We were buying it for $7 to $8 a bottle and selling it for $49.95," said Peterson. "What I didn't understand is a man of [Robertson's] stature putting his name on products like that."

KaloVita distributors slowly began to come forward with stories of how they had lost thousands of dollars when the company refused to refund them for unsold product. When one tried to cash in his inventory the company told him it had "changed its policy"; another, an Indianapolis retiree, was forced to refinance her home.

Finally CBN fessed up. Yes, it had funneled $2.8 million in tax-exempt ministry funds to prop up the failing venture—but Robertson said he would pay it all back personally and reimburse the disgruntled distributors, plus additional promotional costs (and he did).

At the time Gerald Kaufman, cochair of the National Council of Non-Profit Associations, commented, "You don't risk a charity's money. It violates acceptable standards. . . . It seems to me that [Robertson is] treating this ministry as his own. He doesn't own it. In a sense, the public owns it. He's just a trustee."

Trackers of Robertson could see that his real mistake was much more elemental: He hadn't kept his customers satisfied. As the preeminent marketer to the evangelical community on *The 700 Club*, Robertson would always deliver. A few more dollars would always buy another perfectly prepared slice of eternal hope. But when Robertson offered a more tangible commodity, in this case cash returns on health-product investments, his customers still expected him to deliver. In 1994, after the scandal broke, Robertson sold the firm to a Dallas company, Royal BodyCare.

Other similar attempts by Robertson to launch quantifiable products with scant relationships to his overarching Christian philosophy have either failed or instigated regulatory ire.

In 1993 Robertson devised Standard News, a daily radio newscast which intended to "provide world and national coverage without prejudging newsmakers and events" for more than 600 outlets. That business and another called ZapNews, a daily fax publication, foundered and were later sold.

(In 1995, Mark A. Barth, former president of the United States Media Corporation, the Robertson-owned parent of Standard News sued his former employer for $3 million, charging that he had been fired after refusing an order from Tim Robertson to "revalue to zero" $9 million in assets that the four-year-old U.S. Media transferred to IFE. Pat Robertson countered with a $12 million mismanagement suit against Barth, who had alleged that Robertson concealed the loss of USMC assets in order to entice Asian businessman Kay Peng Khoo, "who was contemplating investing $10 million in USMC.")

And when the international media focused their sights on Zaire last year, home to a frightful Ebola virus epidemic and the world's most repressive and corrupt dictator, Mobutu Sese Seko, another one of Robertson's ill-conceived ventures was unearthed. Since 1992, the Robertson-owned African Development Company has run diamond-mining and forestry operations in Zaire.

It was Robertson's Operation Blessing that first landed in Zaire to head up an unsuccessful relief effort on a corn farm outside Kinshasa,

Zaire's capital. A later Operation Blessing project in Goma was strongly criticized by other American aid groups for wasting too much money on transport costs and spending too much time proselytizing while more people died.

Pat Robertson has since become Mobutu's most vocal American supporter, arguing that the Clinton administration's refusal since 1993 to grant a U.S. visa to the ruthless leader, who himself subsists on a hefty take from Zaire's largely unregulated $300 million-a-year diamond trade, is "outrageous." Robertson stands alongside Washington conservatives and lobbyists who claim that Mobutu is heading toward democracy even as the country's infrastructure deteriorates further.

All of this suggests that whenever Robertson has abandoned either his beneficent celebrity persona or his muzzy Christian message, his chances for success were slim. His talents as a showman and producer, after all, are formidable.

"You don't know what it's like to do ninety minutes live every day—it's extraordinary," said former *700 Club* producer Gerard Straub, describing his former boss's on-air magnetism. "When you finish doing ninety minutes live with a guy like Pat Robertson, whose mind is so sharp, you just don't walk out and go sit down and say a prayer. You're hyped, you're flying. It's exhilarating stuff. It's like with any other exciting performer—ask anyone who's in showbiz."

———◇———

Despite Robertson's undeniable TV magnetism, he's also had little luck in selling a convincingly moderate portrait of his political self to the American people.

Attempts to sculpt a slick mediagenic image of himself for the electorate during his 1988 presidential campaign fell hard and flat.

As it turned out, reporters delighted in oppugning Robertson's mendacious style of politicking, eagerly poking holes in each paper-thin cartoon rendering of political secularity. Robertson witnessed *The Wall Street Journal* savage his "economist" credential from the esteemed London School of Economics, revealed to be his attendance there for three months during the summer of 1950 in a course of art appreciation designed especially for visiting American students.

Fellow GOP candidates George Bush and Jack Kemp relished mocking Robertson's statement during a televised debate that as president he would get Soviet nuclear missiles out of Cuba. When all knowledgeable sources, including the White House, stated that there was no evidence that Cuba harbored such weapons, Robertson was forced to admit he had no proof of his claim and that it was simply a hunch.

Even the character issue flew right by Robertson when the prenuptial conception of his eldest son Tim became a matter of public record and made a sore identifier for the campaign's premier family values candidate.

Held under the kind of scrutiny that would never be applied to the content of a television program, Robertson's political profile looked uncharacteristically shabby. When challenged on his claim that one could contract AIDS from kissing someone, he refused to elucidate. When asked to entertain perfectly logical queries, such as why he had relieved himself of his ordination or whether it was true that he believed God had told him to run for president, he turned skunk.

Former representative Andy Jacobs Jr., a Democrat from Indiana, recollected for me the events surrounding the libel case filed by Robertson against him and Republican congressman Paul N. "Pete" McCloskey in 1986.

"It's my considered judgment that [Pat Robertson] committed abuse of process," Jacobs said. "He knew the truth—he filed the lawsuit to hang in there through the primaries against Bush. I'm convinced of that."

By the early '80s, Robertson gained a reputation (largely based on his views as expressed on *The 700 Club*) as a bellicose anti-Communist. When Robertson announced his presidential run in 1986, his résumé touted his "combat duty" in Korea as an indispensable prerequisite for the office.

McCloskey, who was wounded in Korea and awarded the Purple Heart, the Navy Cross, and the Silver Star for his service, remembered differently. In January 1951, the USS Breckinridge shipped out from San Diego carrying a battalion of 90 United States Marines toward the front lines of the Korean War, where the Chinese had just attacked. On that transport were Pete McCloskey and Pat Robertson, both second lieutenants.

"Pat was affable, garrulous, and candid," McCloskey wrote in a six-page letter dated August 4, 1986, solicited by his friend Andy Jacobs Jr., who had also been decorated for service in Korea and was concerned about the prospect of a Robertson presidency. "He spoke frankly of his desire to avoid combat and to have his father . . . intervene on his behalf.

"My single distinct memory is of Pat with a big grin on his face," McCloskey's letter continued, "standing on the dock at Kobe . . . saying something like 'So long you guys—good luck,' and telling us that his father had gotten him out of combat duty." Robertson never saw combat, and instead became an assistant adjutant (informally, "liquor officer") at division headquarters in Otsu.

When journalist Robert Novak called Jacobs inquiring about the letter, Jacobs delivered him a photocopy. Novak subsequently published the allegations. Pat Robertson retaliated by slapping McCloskey and Jacobs with a $35 million libel suit. (The judge later excused Jacobs from the suit, saying he had no reason to question the truth of McCloskey's claims.)

Unfortunately for Robertson, the trial was set for March 8, 1988, also known that year as Super Tuesday. Rather than risk public humiliation or at the very least bad publicity, Robertson had the suit dismissed on March 7, even though doing so required him to dismiss "with prejudice."

Robertson's decision mortally wounded his campaign. Many of his supporters couldn't understand why Robertson didn't either admit to the allegations or go to trial with any evidence he might have retained.

Reporters from the *Richmond News Leader* later visited A. Willis Robertson Papers at the College of William and Mary and learned why: Letters penned by the senator revealed the elder Robertson had sought preferential treatment for his son. In one, the senator hailed

General Lemuel Shepherd, the Marine Corps commandant, for "your encouraging message concerning Pat. . . . I am happy he will get some more training before engaging in combat." In another, the Senator informed Dr. Francis P. Gaines, then president of Washington and Lee, that his son Edwin, a friend of Pat's, had also been let off. "Pat and Edwin will be going to an interesting and historical part of Japan," Robertson assured Gaines.

—◁○▷—

In my mind Pat Robertson cannot be faulted for embarking on these minor deflorations of the public's trust in the name of his common good. Neoliberals like me believe that the freedom to spin is as First Amendment–sanctioned as any other mode of speech.

Robertson is correct when he complains about being held to a higher standard than his less ideologically inclined contemporaries. He's also enough of a player to know that harping on such fracases diverts the gaze from his distinctly laissez-faire management style.

In the late '70s, Robertson assigned longtime CBN employee Bob Slosser, a former assistant national editor at *The New York Times,* the formidable task of starting up a full-fledged news broadcast for the network. "Pat just gets on the air and says we're going to have news," recalled one insider. "That's just how things happened, that's how prophets and visionaries do it."

Inspired by CBS's popular *Bicentennial Minute* as well as the utter lack of a news budget, Robertson's producer hired a former used-car salesman named Bob Trotter to read a minute's worth of news torn fresh off a UPI teletype machine each day. In the same way CBS had used its news staff in 1976 to produce an extra minute of content each day to celebrate 200 years of American history (and to sell an extra commercial space), CBN carved its news minute out of *The 700 Club* staff's eight-hour workday.

Years later, CBN News flourishes, with bureaus in Washington and Jerusalem to fire up a daily half-hour of *The 700 Club,* called "Newswatch Today," with convincing simulacra of conventional newscasts. (In 1992, Robertson hoped to augment his mainstream news coverage by purchasing United Press International for $6 million, but decided against the deal once his money men examined the ailing news agency's balance books.)

Mel White considered the six months he spent writing Pat Robertson's 1985 book *America's Date With Destiny* as a real lesson in the art of macromanagement. Robertson had come up with the title, White with the idea to map out the dates in history that his author held were most important. Robertson loved it. "He said, 'You get the dates, you decide the important ones, and then just run them past me,' " White recalled.

"So I started chasing him around the nation, staying in hotel rooms next to his hotel room and sitting for two days, three days," said White. "Finally, in New Orleans, he stopped long enough to have me come to his suite and I said, Well, what would you like me to change? And he said, Oh, I haven't read it yet, I thought we'd read it aloud together." After White politely declined, Robertson agreed to quickly scan the manuscript that night.

Robertson—apparently confident that his ghostwriter had a handle on the project meant to define his perspective for the presidential election—didn't get around to reading his book until after it was published. "It's a real sign of his brilliance that he comes up with so much stuff and hasn't gotten into deeper trouble because of the quality control," White said.

Anecdotes like these convince me that Robertson set sail early on a runnel of spin control that has only recently trickled its way into the mainstream of American discourse. Pat Robertson can hardly be blamed for the condition, only admired for the skillfulness with which he has exploited it.

Fierce spin control at both ends of the political spectrum in our time has made each side appear less credible. "The world of spin is one in which no one can dare take another's words or actions at face value," Eric Alterman wrote recently in *Mother Jones*. "This malleability is one reason our politics have ceased to have much relationship to governance."

At the left of the spectrum are so-called liberals who regard with suspicion any public uprising that disputes the legitimacy of the heterodox status quo. Cited examples include the recent resurgence of proponents for teaching the creationist perspective in public schools, the intermittent third-party presidential campaigning of H. Ross Perot, and the rise of state militia movements and alleged domestic terrorists like Timothy McVeigh and the Unabomber.

At the right are so-called conservatives, who, if they are economic conservatives, cry for less government, and if they are social conservatives, yearn to rescue American culture from its most freewheeling instincts. Both conservative wings might legitimately cite the revolts against school prayer, religious displays in public places, and pro-lifers as restrictive and distressing developments.

On both sides paranoia runs deep—and with good reason. History is rife with examples of demagogic radicals who hoodwinked the general public, however briefly, to deleterious effect.

Liberals will cite examples of conservatism run amuck. In 1954, the Gallup poll reported that 50 percent of Americans held a "favorable opinion" of Joseph McCarthy. By that time, the rapacious Republican senator from Wisconsin had already spuriously accused public figures of every stripe of being "communists," and thus ruined many a life and career. He had also charged both the Truman and Eisenhower administrations with "treason." According to the same Gallup poll, only 29 percent of Americans at the time held an "unfavorable opinion" of McCarthy.

In 1994, Republicans captured majorities in both houses of Congress for the first time since 1952; Democrats quaked in their boots, hoping out loud that the changing of the guard didn't signal a sharp, malevolent turn to the right for America. Is the Republican revolution more or less a threat than McCarthyism?

Pat Robertson, in his 1993 book *The Turning Tide,* supplies the negative results of leftist radicalism, "curses" he calls them, that have briefly besieged our nation. "In Vietnam," he wrote, "for the first time in America's history, our armed forces were defeated in major war, a war whose beginning coincided with the Supreme Court decision to ban God from our public schools."

Today, Robertson lamented, the U.S. economy is reliant on foreign sources for at least 50 percent of its petroleum, a result of an oil crisis which "took place the same year our Supreme Court legalized the murder of unborn babies."

The issues alluded to in all the above examples are real issues. It's just that in the current cultural climate whether or not any of these perspectives appeals to you depends a lot more on what you already believe in than the merits of the claims.

Pat Robertson's successive power as media titan is evidence of just how unsatisfactory labels like *conservative* and *liberal* have become. Anybody who engages in today's public ideological battles solely to further their openly stated partisan agenda is playing a fool's game. In today's internecine political climate, the real winners are the people who profit no matter what their party's outcome.

Pat Robertson's genuine religious trappings make it difficult for millions of Americans to find fault in his motives. "People have a very superficial positiveness toward religion," reasoned Edmund Cohen, a Robertson watchdog and author of *The Mind of the Bible-Believer.* "There is a taboo against attacking organized religion directly, so there is a difficulty getting even journalists over that taboo when there's a religious figure who has this much potential for harm."

It's no wonder Robertson is constantly barraging his viewers with tirades against radical African-American leader Louis Farrakhan. Were it not for Farrakhan's race (black) and religion (Islam), he'd resemble no leader so much as Pat Robertson.

Back at the Century Plaza Hotel, I was feeling more than a little skeptical about the doomsaying omens of the Robertson watchdogs. It had not been lost on me that the most vitriolic of these messengers had been affiliated either with Robertson or the conservative Christian movement at some point in their life-spans. Loosed from the discernments of a religious-based morality, I didn't see how Pat Robertson could be accused of engaging in public bricolage any more reprehensible than that of a cutthroat CEO at a Fortune 500 company.

Let's just say you're never going to find the members of the Montana militia sporting evening wear and chomping down lobster tails to the finest in overripe dinner entertainment Hollywood has to offer.

Robertson is held to a higher standard precisely because he traffics in the judgment of others. In this context, every perceived moral slipup is a slap in the face to those who want to believe. For everyone else, it's comic relief.

In the only major gaffe of the evening, the stage crew began packing up the stage before Heather Whitestone, the first deaf Miss America, began her ballet finale. Although much of the audience was already headed for the door, the proper equipment was reconnected and Whitestone executed her clumsy modern dance routine, playing every bit the part of a wounded white dove, in one of the evening's rare drab moments.

The show came to a close at about 11:30, after which Pat and Dede mingled in the roped-off VIP area. Fifteen minutes later, Robertson was escorted out a back door by a radio-rigged security guard.

By this time I'm waxing a little more sympathetic to Robertson and his mission than I'd like to be. Frankly, I've started to feel like the university professor played by William Hurt in the movie *Altered States*. Remember the scene where he's banging himself as hard as he can against the walls to prevent himself from transforming into a blobby homunculus? Robertson's spell is unrelenting.

A level up, at the hotel's piano bar, I suddenly feel a little better. A couple of roasters are already ordering scotch and sodas. I even spotted a few younger members of the retinue light up cigarettes. The real California, the one of sun and fun, couldn't help but bare its bitchin' bod.

But Pat Robertson and California aren't as incongruous as one might think.

The Golden State, after all, is home to the California Independent Business PAC, an Orange County–based political action group formed by five conservative Christian multimillionaires—Howard Ahmanson Jr., Rob Hurtt, Richard Riddle, Roland Hinz, and Edward Atsinger III—that has bankrolled the campaigns of more than 50 percent of the Republicans in the California assembly and state senate since it was founded (as the Allied Business PAC) in 1991. (Atsinger purchased the Christian Broadcasting radio network from Robertson in 1992 and renamed it the Salem Radio Network.)

Then there's Sara DeVito Hardman, who in 1991 formed the California affiliate of the Christian Coalition in Tarzana. Hardman, who is also an active member of the 8,000-member Church on the Way, has helped build the Christian Coalition of California into a powerful group that claims 150,000 members, the largest in any state.

Last April, Hardman was elected a member of the secretive Council on National Policy.

The rarely written-about Council on National Policy is another group that might cause one to reassess Robertson's relationship to mainstream: It first convened in 1981 at the McLean, Virginia, home of conservative direct-mail strategist Richard Viguerie; formed by Viguerie, Texas oil millionaire T. Cullen Davis, and San Diego minister/conservative activist Tim La Haye, among others, the group consciously set about to be the ultraconservative alternative to what its members considered to be similar but liberal organizations like the Trilateral Commission and the Council on Foreign Relations.

The CNP has met three times a year every year since, in gatherings that are notorious for being closed to the press (this spring one was held in Orlando, Florida). To anyone who might have thought the political turbine of the radical right stalled with the disbanding of the Moral Majority, the CPR's member list would read as something of a fright: Joseph Coors, Herbert and Nelson Bunker Hunt, Phyllis Schlafly, Oliver North, Paul Weyrich, Howard Phillips, James Dobson, Gary Bauer, and James Watt have all been members.

Pat Robertson was president of the Council on National Policy from 1985 to 1986.

In short, the Council on National Policy sounds an awful lot like a prototype for the kind of organization Robertson forever warns his readers and viewers about: an unregulated cabal of partisan elites who are plotting the fate of the world behind closed doors.

——◦——

In the end Pat Robertson resembles no one so much as Woody Allen's character Zelig, the chameleon-like celebrity who pops up at the borders of major world events, appearing totally at home and yet strangely unrecognizable to those who surround him.

Last October Robertson stood alongside Pope John Paul II on a stage in New York during the pontiff's visit and informed him in a private meeting at John Cardinal O'Connor's residence that "while there are doctrinal differences that separate us, I strongly believe the moral crisis facing society today and the obvious social breakdown mandate a closer cooperation between people of faith, including Evangelicals and Catholics."

What was he doing there? The same month, the Christian Coalition had announced the formation of the Catholic Alliance, an adjunct organization intended to coax support and money from conservative members of America's largest religious denomination.

Perhaps conservative Catholics, a crucial swing vote in 1996, were a natural Robertson ally, yet the initial backlash was not encouraging.

"No group has the right to appropriate the name 'Catholic' for itself, wrongly implying that it has the official stamp of approval from the church," responded Bishop Walter F. Sullivan of Richmond, Virginia. Bishops in Colorado issued a similar missive asserting that while they and the Christian Coalition sometimes agreed on issues like abortion, euthanasia, and pornography, "we sharply disagree on issues such as welfare reform, capital punishment, and health care reform."

Again, Robertson had failed to exert influence outside his core evangelical consumer base. For all his myriad efforts to win ironclad reputations as an educator, a religious prophet, a political prognosticator, a man of ideas, Robertson was still regarded most highly in the field that had always upheld his other interests: business.

Ironically, it's only within the morality-free corridors of commerce that Pat Robertson has ever convincingly played the part of the putative sage. Only in the framework of *The 700 Club*—at this juncture, essentially the world's longest-running infomercial—can Robertson air "wisdoms" like this pearl from an early 1994 show:

I do believe this year that there're going to be persecutions against Christians. I think that the government is going to step up its attacks against Christians this year 1994. And it's the kind of thing where the Lord is going to protect us if we pray. It was like Peter who was taken prisoner but the church was praying for him, and I think that prayers are going to be extremely important in 1994. But I do think that the government, frankly, is our enemy. And we're going to see more and more of the people who've been placed in office last year are kind of getting what they call their sea legs, they're getting control of the levers of power, and they will begin to know how to use them, and they'll use them to hurt those who are perceived as their enemies.

Hermetically sealed off from the harsh judgments of his critics, Robertson can spin such anarchic rhetoric as commonsense homily. The profits of The Family Channel, which is bound by its bylaws to broadcast *The 700 Club* ad infinitum, artificially sustain a program that can make its costs only by spending the bulk of its viewers' charitable contributions (70 percent, according to some estimates).

Congressman Fortney Pete Stark, a Democrat from California, came to a similar conclusion before introducing legislation in November 1993 intended to hit Robertson where it counted—in his money belt. Stark, a member of the House Ways and Means Committee, proposed a penalty excise tax of up to 200 percent on the excess gains made available to insiders when nonprofit companies turn profit. "Individuals have enriched themselves at the public's expense while nonprofit organizations have been looted," Stark averred from the House floor.

Whether or not Stark's legislation passes, it's not likely to have much of an effect on Pat Robertson's empire. For one, the Robertsons and their fellow investors have already reaped the benefits of the IFE buyout transaction. Furthermore, Robertson continues to provide his customers with the familiar, digestible product they have come to rely on.

And it would take nothing short of a total overhaul of the beleaguered Internal Revenue Service's nonprofit rules to sever the bizarre but currently legal relationship between *The 700 Club* and International Family Entertainment.

Besides, superficial notions like celebrity and image have their way of prevailing over deep-seeming ethical platitudes in American society. And I'm all for it. Our modern media, with their cool, nonjudgmental nature, are the ultimate democratizing force, at the service of anyone who can master them and use them to push society's pleasure buttons. If Pat Robertson can do it, those who oppose him can, too. I'll take action movies and fast food over someone else's morality any day.

Pop artist Andy Warhol once said, "If you want to know all about Andy Warhol, just look at the surface: of my paintings and films and me, and there I am. There's nothing behind it." Pat Robertson, through his spokesman Gene Kapp, told me pretty much the same thing. He did not wish to be interviewed for this book. I was also officially prohibited from talking to any IFE employees. Kapp explained to me that Robertson had cooperated with other book authors in the past and hadn't been pleased with the results (an odd comment considering they've all been favorable).

As it turned out, I didn't really need Robertson himself. As with Andy Warhol, Pat Robertson has created a body of work so vibrant and proliferative that it blots out his comparatively bland personal traits. Pat Robertson has proscribed a whole world—a true-blue fantasia where there is a simple solution to every problem. ("There have always been big questions in life," reads the cover line on Robertson's book *Answers to 200 of Life's Most Probing Questions*. "Now there are answers to match.")

What, then, if anything, can one learn from Pat Robertson's vast oeuvre?

First, resist stereotyping people whose views you disagree with. Pat Robertson made millions off of what his supporters believe to be a flagrant disregard for their viewpoint and concerns. Ignore opposing those viewpoints at your own peril: Many of Robertson's supporters are as upscale, well-educated, and as well-to-do as their mainstream counterparts.

Second, regard powerful people who call themselves "outsiders" with the same healthy suspicion reserved for career power-mongers. Pat Robertson's genteel roots and lubricity within establishment conservative circles stand directly at odds with his pose as a man of the people.

Third, gather news and information from a wide variety of sources. Pat Robertson knows the strengths and weaknesses of different media formats. Although different aspects of his rise to a position of power and influence have been expertly chronicled over the years, both in print and on television, no one source has accurately circumscribed the farthest reaches of Robertson's empire for an appreciably large audience.

Fourth, embrace technology. If you don't, someone else will— and may end up wielding it against you. By remaining at the vanguard of the technological revolution for the past 20 years, Pat Robertson has frequently had first dibs on the latest in communications hardware. Powerful tools of communication allow minority interests to greatly amplify whatever message they choose and thus create an artificially inflated impression of their infrastructure.

Fifth, watch the ball. The real news about Pat Robertson is not his political or religious opinions, but rather the way in which the aggregate sum of his wealth, power, and influence enables him to infuse American culture, and those that look to it for guidance, with those opinions.

———◁◦▷———

Ralph Reed Jr., executive director of Pat Robertson's Christian Coalition, often refers to a distressing "coarsening of our culture," which presumably must be sanded smooth and polished to a high gloss if we're ever to move forward as a civilization. I know what he means.

The other day I walked past a Family Channel advertisement tacked to the side of a phone booth in New York. "Just watch us now," it proclaimed. And then in bold type, under the fluid, cartoon-shiny Family Channel logo, were the words "America's fastest growing cable channel."

The epigraph to Pat Robertson's 1972 autobiography quotes from Matthew and reads in part: "There is nothing covered up / That will not be uncovered, / Nothing hidden / That will not be made known." In that spirit of total disclosure I present the following thoughts:

How many people noticed that sign each day and gave The Family Channel a brief positive thought because of it? Maybe a young parent saw it and thought, I'm glad there's finally a wholesome TV station I can always watch with kids. Perhaps an ad executive caught a glimpse of it and made a mental note to call the burgeoning network for a media kit the next morning. Had a preteen been drawn to it by the bright Technicolor logo and wondered whether the network aired fun shows for kids? Or a senior citizen looking for old reruns from the fifties?

And of those potential thousands (the ad, after all, was displayed on a bustling Manhattan street corner), how many knew about the man who founded The Family Channel?

Did they know that in Pat Robertson's world "family values" meant "born-again Christian values"? That Pat Robertson had on numerous occasions referred to computer bar codes as "the mark of the Beast," referred to in Revelation 14:9–11? That Pat Robertson once wrote "I firmly expect to be alive when Jesus Christ comes back to earth"? Or that he advised that the religious beliefs of Mormons were "wrong" and that Hinduism was a "cult"?

Would they think any differently if they knew that Pat Robertson regarded the mainstream's gradual acceptance of homosexuals, whom he said the New Testament had sentenced to death, as an indication that our society was in its final stages of decay? That this man who counsels against a conspiracy toward one-world government has himself spent his life sowing the seeds for a self-styled evangelical global takeover?

Perhaps some of them would agree with and endorse Robertson's plan. And others would no doubt disagree. But the majority probably would never give the matter a second thought, until the next time they flipped on their televisions and began to channel-surf. They might have scanned for The Family Channel, in search of some good old-fashioned entertainment. And they just might happen upon *The 700 Club,* where a kindly, distinguished gentleman would offer them a prayer and some words of advice on the matters of the day. And then explain in the even, patrician tones of a Virginia long gone how the whole wide world would soon come crashing down and explode into flames.

But for just a few dollars a month, maybe a little more than they thought they could afford, they might rest easy. Knowing that they had extended the reach for a voice of hope, a beacon of righteousness, the prophet of the new world order.

Talk about coarse.

INDEX